D1927672

Global Warning

Prophetic Details Revealed

Bill Vincent

© 2016 by Bill Vincent.

All rights reserved. No part of this book may be reproduced, stored in a retrieval system or transmitted in any form or by any means without the prior written permission of the publishers, except by a reviewer who may quote brief passages in a review to be printed in a newspaper, magazine or journal.

Softcover 978-0692699171

Hardcover 978-1-60796-971-6

PUBLISHED BY REVIVAL WAVES OF GLORY BOOKS & PUBLISHING

www.revivalwavesofglory.com

Litchfield, IL

Printed in the United States of America

Table of Contents

Introduction

I'm going to start this out by laying a foundation of what God is talking about concerning Sound the Alarm. We are to be Watchman of the Lord and God is raising us up to be watchman.

Over the summer we were having meetings in the park in Litchfield, IL and God spoke specifically to our Ministry "Revival Waves of Glory" and He said that we were to rise up as watchman of the Lord. We are to be those who stand and watch and see in the Spirit and be able to speak truth. We are to take a stand on behalf of America. The real red, white and blue would bleed through those who stand as real watchman of the Lord. God is raising up the ministry to be like these men and women of God. I'm telling you in the midst of doing this we did not know what to do with it at the time so we just put it on the shelf and then December 31st 2012 we released a Word of the Lord for 2013. God specifically spoke that He wanted to do a Sound the Alarm Conference and He gave us a date of February 23rd-25th 2013. This was prophesied and we are doing what God said. We had the conference in the midst of an eight month long Revival at Waves of Revival Belleville, IL. You need to understand it's not about us it's about doing what we have to do. This is a critical hour and we've got to understand what a Watchman is. God is also going to have me talk about Gatekeepers. God spoke that there was a gate over this region and this gate was being unlatched and beginning to open. One thing I want you to understand is that we have to have gatekeepers as well. In other words we have to keep watch of what's going and coming from Heaven, because not only does good come and go from Heaven but evil comes and goes from the second Heaven.

We have to understand that there have been things happening in America that the Church has just winked at. We have just winked at it. We haven't really taken a stand. Oh yes there has been some picketing by certain Christian people. They will stand out side with a sign and say this is wrong here and there. But how many know we have to rise up a lot more than just a picket sign. I'm not talking about burning people's barns down. We don't have to deal with flesh and blood. We are dealing with principalities, powers and wickedness in high places. After today, I'm not going out with picket signs and I'm not going to do this and that. What I'm going to do is take authority and speak this out into the world there is going to be a supernatural taking hold of the Church rising up in this hour and uniting to together. Putting away childish things and putting away nitpicking things that are just getting in the way where the Church is concerned. To begin to realize no matter what denomination you are from we all can unite together and pray for a purpose and that is a safety of our Nation. That is the safety of the United States of America.

The Church has used a blind eye when it comes to politicians and when it comes to voting. People vote because their candidate is good looking. I did not know that is what we were voting for. This is not President of sixth grade. Come on this is voting for the President of the United States. We are not supposed to vote because the candidate is black or white. It's gotten to the place that people vote for black, white, Jewish and even Republican and Democrat doesn't mean anything any more. It's about rather they are right in God's sight or not. We have to release this because we are coming upon judgment day and what I mean by that is not the last Day of Judgment where God judges us all. I'm talking about God is about to judge the earth. Only God's favored, God's anointed and God's people are going to be lifted to a higher standard. They also will be blessed beyond riches. The favor of the Lord is going to be put upon God's people in the midst of all kinds of chaos, wars, fighting's and rumors of wars according to the Bible. These things will be taking place and God's people will be put in the safe hand of God. No one is going to be able to penetrate the favored of the Lord. This is what God is about to raise up in this hour.

9-11 was supposed to be a wake up call and the Nation of the United States is already dropping the ball we would be exposed right now if we would be attacked. When Japan attacked us we dropped the ball and it was a wake up call. Many years later we get attacked again and the World Trade Centers fall, thousands are killed and it's another wake up call. All we do is tighten up things for a while and then we loosen it up again to be exposed to another power.

Let me tell you there are some things I will talk about as well that have to do with Israel. We would not have many of the things going on in America if we would back Israel the way we are supposed to. If the President would take a stand with Israel and say that no matter what we are not going to allow anyone to take any more of their land. I have specific quotes out of the mouth of this man and we are going to talk about some of this stuff. President Obama has said some things and we have to take a stand where he hasn't even stood behind his own words. If you say well "I'm pro Obama" well then you are not going to like me to much. Listen it's not about Republican or Democrat. It's about right or wrong. It's about what's going on in the Bible and how they line up. When I vote I do not go by anything but beliefs now. I have to vote for the lesser of two evils. Why? Because you can't get a Politian who believes right. Mickey Mouse would have better luck in the White House right now. What are we supposed to consider when we go vote? One is abortion, another should be freedom of religion and another one is same sex marriage. Obama and other Presidents have taken away from freedom of religion. The Laws are changing to where Churches of a certain status cannot preach certain things. If they do they can lose their status, Church or even get a hefty fine. That is the same as communism. Same sex marriage we already know where Obama stands on that. There have been more of these types of weddings over the last ten years. I can't just blame

Obama. Then we get to the next one abortion. There is more legalized abortion and the morning after pill. Why don't we just give mothers a gun and let them kill their babies if they don't want them. What about the dumpster baby dumps? This is the United States of America where freedom is supposed to reign. We are supposed to be men and women of valor; we were established of God and Godly principles in God We Trust and we are now a Nation of hypocritic (Hypocrites) oath. I meant to say that.

We are going to understand some things and we are going to get into some things. I want you to understand before I get into it. I don't watch the news all year long. I don't look for news. I don't watch about Israel. God told me that we were going to have this conference and I didn't even begin to press in for it until the week of. All this time all I was getting is Words of Knowledge. God would speak a Word and I would write it down. The week of the Conference I sat down and sought the Lord concerning Words He had spoken and it all unfolded for what He wanted to speak concerning Sounding the Alarm. Alarmists are always looking for an alarm. A real Watchman watches and waits in the Spirit. We could watch the News and get stirred real quickly. I could watch the news for a half hour and have all kinds of sermons. It's not about stirring my soul up to release this stuff. I'm not that kind of preacher. I love to preach about Revival and prophesy about what God's going to do but it is time to Sound the Alarm directed by the Holy Spirit.

Even the Word of the Lord for 2013 was more powerful

than any I've ever released. It had more punch in it. So we will begin by laying a foundation before we get into all the stuff God has spoken.

Please don't read ahead to see the stuff. You need the foundational things to receive the prophetic truths released.

Watchman of the Lord

What is a watchman? We have to understand what this is all about so we can receive. You don't want all of this to fall on dead ground. Some of the things that we will talk about concerning our Nation have been exposed to us as a Body of Christ. I don't blame the President, I blame the Church. If you want to blame anybody it's the Churches fault. If the Church would take a stand for America the Nation would change. One by one God has spoken of things that America has opened up to the enemy. The anti-christ spirit is moving in America. I'm not talking about the final man that shall rise up as the devil himself in the flesh called the anti-christ.

Are you ready?

Does a watchman watch television and world events to tell people of incoming warnings? This is not a watchman. Some are so busy looking for media venues, they miss the point. What is the definition of a watchman as GOD.?

Ezekiel 33:7 So thou, O son of man, I have set thee a watchman unto the house of Israel; therefore thou shalt hear the word at my mouth, and warn them from me.

God has even spoke to me concerning food items that are deadly. One of those items is Stevia and sugar substitute. God said this stuff does not agree with the body. It gets in the arteries and clogs up and gradually kills a person. There are many side effects if taken in large doses. It is like a poison. It is advertised as a natural substitute to sugar but there is more according to God. God said what is your body mostly made up of? Water…. This Stevia does not dissolve in water. God said it lines the lining of the stomach to eat away much like a acid. He said this has already caused death to dogs that have eaten this. He took me to a Yahoo News ad that showed dogs ate stuff with Stevia and died. Safe I don't think so. A friend had offered this stuff to me before I knew it was bad. I took a drink and God spoke to me "you just drank poison." I got an email from a Pastor whom had found his dog dead and all he could see was Stevia box chewed open.

This is not even anything I had planned to release but evidently someone needs to hear this. There are many products I may talk about in the coming months that God told me not to have anymore.

A watchman for the Lord is someone who spends time in His Presence and in prayer to wait for His Word to give warnings to His people.

I have been processing what God has been speaking for months and now is the time for releasing.

So many people are ready to release a warning but their warning is not from God it's from the soul realm. Specifically Television Ministers, buy this barrel of food because the world is going to end. That is a soul realm warning. You have to buy their barrels of food and filters that will filter your toilet water. Preachers on Television are putting fear across the world. They are selling millions of dollars of product to support their Television Ministry. I don't say this to put them down. I say this because it comes from the fear of the soul realm. It's not from their thus saith the Lord you know why, because many of them said Jesus was going to return in 2012. I want to get ready for the end of the world by the supernatural power of God. I want the supernatural manna from Heaven and the Heavens opening up to supply everything I need. To be able to see water flow from a rock by the power of God's Glory. I don't want to stock pile a bunch of food out of fear. The food only last so long and then what? If you have bought into this fear all you have to do is repent. I say all this because they feed on the fears of America and it all comes from their soul realm. In other words it is not the Spirit. The Soul is in the flesh realm. We need it of the Holy Spirit. Now if God was warning us, there would be a bigger warning. The thing is some of the warnings that have come; most of them didn't have a clue on 911. If they were really hearing from God don't you think they would have had a clue? You know the first thing I said when 911 took place? I said God forgive me. Could I have manipulated my prophetic Words to look like I knew it was going to happen? I probably could but I'm not going to. I just want to say God I want to make sure I hear you next time. I don't want to miss it. I want to know that I know that I know.

Ezekiel 33:3 If when he seeth the sword come upon the

land, he blow the trumpet, and warn the people;

What does the trumpet represent? Blow the trumpet!!!

Exodus 19:16 And it came to pass on the third day in the morning, that there were thunders and lightnings, and a thick cloud upon the mount, and the voice of the trumpet exceeding loud; so that all the people that *was* in the camp trembled.

Revelations 4:1 After this I looked, and, behold, a door *was* opened in heaven: and the first voice which I heard *was* as it were of a trumpet talking with me; which said, Come up hither, and I will shew thee things which must be hereafter.

The trumpet is God's VOICE!!!

This is the day that we need to stand together and hear the trumpet of the Lord. Right now the Church wouldn't know the trumpet sound if it bit them in the butt. We have to hear and we have to be obedient. Listen and Heed to His Reproof as it is blown. Turn from your Sins and Repent. Return to your First Love. Return and turn to Him now in your comfort. The trumpet is blowing. He is warning His Church to wake up! Wake up Bride of Christ. Wake up from your slumber.

God said to me "Lazarus is just sleeping and my Church is Lazarus. Lazarus was sleeping. He sleepeth and stinketh because he is dead". The Church is dead and God says, "Lazarus come forth.... Wake up from your slumber

Church. Separate yourselves from the world. Walk in His Commandments and in Holiness."

Isaiah 21:6 For thus hath the Lord said unto me, Go, set a watchman, let him declare what he seeth.

The Church is almost to a place that they should be ashamed of themselves. I'm not releasing shame upon the Church but the Church as a whole is still living as though Jesus is still on the cross and that Jesus has not risen when He has. Are we going to be a Church that speaks truth? Are we going to be a Church that doesn't pet demons? Are we going to be a Church that doesn't take any mercy on the enemy? We are supposed to take a stand as a Church in this hour. The Church as I see it prophetically is a Church of weakness and constantly not doing as God says.

Gatekeepers and Watchmen!

You are to speak out The Lord has called you to be bold today. The Church has been spineless. We can have something going on in our own Church and we don't want to speak up. Oh we got to please the givers and we got to make the tithers happy. It doesn't matter how much someone gives, we cannot ignore sin in the house of God.

Gatekeepers Have Roles

Protect the Lord's House

There are not enough people really wanting to protect the Lord's House. We let someone with demonic spirits comes in and mess up what we work to keep pure. We have to take a stand. When certain spirits come in the Church you have to deal with it. People don't want to create waves so they leave the spirits alone. We love waves at Revival WAVES of Glory. I'm not talking about the new born again children of God. We get a lot more grace when we are young in the Lord. Many Churches don't want sinners to come when we must accept all sinners. Sinners who come to Church will be set free. Most of the most critical Christians are the one's full of pet demons they don't want anyone to know about.

Protect the Lord's House means they defend the gospel, the truth of the Word and protect the holiness of God's house. Their hearts are on fire with the Fear of the Lord.

Some people see my wife and I as over protective of certain things. First of all we are one of the freest Ministries you will ever know. When it comes to the Holy Spirit being grieved you become my enemy. Some Churches have become cool aid parties.

The protectors want the Lord's house to be a house of Prayer and they are not content until they see the Lord's will come to the house of God. The gatekeeper protects the House. They know the scriptures well and are full of understanding. They are bold to speak out against the sins of the church-even if it means they will be mocked, hated or even kicked out of the church. They stay close to the House of the Lord.

The stand I took in 2010 to walk out in the midst of Revival was me taking a stand as a watchman of the Lord. I did not know all that was going on there in Litchfield, IL until I walked out from under that influence. It was a decision God made through me not to allow the hypocrisy to continue and I wasn't going to support it any longer. They can say whatever they want and they did. They can do whatever they want and they did that too. But as far as me and my house we are going to serve the Lord and He is going to be the center of attention. There is not going to be some person lifted higher than God and that is what happened there.

We have to understand this, is there anyone among us whom will take a stand as a watchman.

They keep the Lord's People on the Right Path

As a staff or sheepdog would keep the sheep together from straying, so the role of gatekeeper is the same. We need Pastors who are Sheppard's. I would have blood on my hands if I just winked at sin. The Gatekeeper is responsible to oversee the people, gently guide the drifter back and keep those on the threshold of evil paths from taking another step in the wrong direction. They are bold and not afraid to tell the truth of God's word, knowing full well they are saving many from the fires of eternal hell. They are prayer warriors and intercessors for the people.

I've had many ministers join my ministry and then they tithe to my ministry and then they try to control how I do things. God is my source so I do not have to worry about their tithes. If we are going to be Gatekeepers we are not to be moved by money but preaching the truth, the whole truth and nothing but the truth. If we do not use the rod to guide the sheep the rod will be turned back on us. The rod works both ways. If we don't take a stand we will have blood on our hands. You know I would hate for anyone who's been in my services to end up in the pit of hell, because I did not tell them the full truth.

On a side note: If I hear one more Minister or Television Evangelist say the comment once saved always saved, I'm going to scream. It's an abomination and a lie from the pit of hell. They say that if you ask Jesus into your heart you are saved forever. You never have to repent, you never have to ask for forgiveness you are clean forever. That is a lie. They preach it and sell books about it. They are famous and Church is packed. Do you know why? Because the Church is seeker friendly.

They Keep Watch for the Master's Return Ready to usher in the King of Glory.

Some believe they get to live how they want and we all go to Heaven. This is not true. Even the book and Movie of the Left Behind Series show people being left behind but this is not the way it's going to be. This is not scriptural.

Who is a Gatekeeper?

According to the Old Testament, a gatekeeper was a Levite. Gatekeepers were also watchmen on the walls. They were ministering priests from the tribe of Levi. Gatekeepers were trusted officials and high priests in the servant role of protecting the Lord's house. They were stationed at all 4 gates (N, S, E, W). They also appointed and taught others around them to guard the gate as well. Their hearts were fully committed to the Lords will. Today's gatekeepers hope and pray for revival and eagerly await the Lord's return. God told me that if a Watchman is not praying for Revival then they are not a Gatekeeper.

Gatekeepers are always prepared and continually remind others to be ready. Gatekeepers made sure that nothing unholy entered into God's house and nothing was allowed to leave unless it had approval. They were in charge of the Temple items and treasuries of the House of the Lord.

Running Away from This is Not an Option

(Jonah didn't win) You are commanded to speak out and warn them pay attention:

The Lord's Message came to me: "Son of man, speak to your people. Tell them, If I bring war on this land and the people take one of their citizens and make him their **watchman**, and if the watchman sees war coming and blows the trumpet, warning the people, then if anyone hears the sound of the trumpet and ignores it and war comes and takes him off, it's his own fault. He heard the alarm, he ignored it—it's his own fault. If he had listened, he would have saved his life. But if the watchman sees war coming and doesn't blow the trumpet, warning the people, and war comes and takes anyone off, I'll hold the watchman responsible for the bloodshed of any unwarned sinner."

Let's talk about 9-11 for a bit. Many people called in sick that terrible day. I met a man and prophesied to him saying, "You blame yourself for many whom died but he needs to just thank God that he survived." He came up to me after the service and showed me his plane ticket; he was supposed to be on one of the planes. I believe many who died that day; it was not their time. Their death was a robbery from the pit of hell. Whether you like it or not; the devil stole people's lives that day. Many of those who died probably were reserved a special place in Heaven for being martyred by an evil war attack. (God only knows) Hundreds of Firefighters died and rescue crews digging in the rubble. Many of the Firefighter whom survived are dying today from cleaning up that mess. It's like there is still a curse upon their lives. Families whom had to go to many funerals of their fallen comrades will continue to go to funerals of the sick rescue crews today. No one can justify that. Our Nation still has not fully recovered from 911. I know it's been a long time now. I'm not trying to parade on 911. I'm not saying this for any benefit. I say this because America Sleeps while hell reaps. The explosions stopped, the crumbling stopped, monuments have been built, there have been all kinds of parades, ceremonies, name plates, engraved signs and television specials.... What about the people still dying, because of the wounds inside their hearts. What about the people who got cancer from the debris that they had to clean up or dig bodies and parts of bodies out. The thing is New York and the United States are not helping the families like they should. If a member of war dies the family just gets a couple hundred bucks a month. My old Pastor lost his leg in Vietnam and the Government only gave him couple thousand dollars. I say this because; don't fall asleep in the midst of wars. Imagine if that happened in every State in America. The picture on the cover of this book is America on fire with explosions. I wanted this graphic picture because this is what the Church has done to our Country if we don't rise up we will all see it. The Church sleeps while gross evil is covering the earth. There are things in the rest of this book some will try to down play but if God says they are a big deal then they are a big deal.

"You, son of man, are the watchman. I've made you a watchman for Israel. The minute you hear a message from me, warn them. If I say to the wicked, 'Wicked man, wicked woman, you're on the fast track to death!' and you don't speak up and warn the wicked to change their ways, the wicked will die unwarned in their sins and I'll hold you responsible for their bloodshed. But if you warn the wicked to change their ways and they don't do it, they'll die in their sins well-warned and at least you will have saved your own life."

"Son of man, I've made you a watchman for Israel. Whenever you hear me say something, warn them for me. If I say to the wicked, 'You are going to die,' and you don't sound the alarm warning them that it's a matter of life or death, they will die and it will be your fault. I'll hold you responsible. But if you warn the wicked and they keep right on sinning anyway, they'll most certainly die for their sin, but you won't die. You'll have saved your life." And if the righteous turn back from living righteously and take up with evil when I step in and put them in a hard place, they'll die. If you haven't warned them, they'll die because of their sins, and none of the right things they've done will count for anything—and I'll hold you responsible. But if you warn these righteous people not to sin and they listen to you, they'll live because they took the warning—and again, you'll have saved your life.

Gatekeeper's Role of Protecting the People

The gatekeepers of these last days have been commissioned to protect the sheep. You are to devote yourselves to holiness and to protect the sheep. We can no longer fear what man thinks, what he may say, do, or even notice their countenance – Fear God and what lies ahead for all of us. Take your stand and don't turn to look around to the right or left, who cares what people think-ask yourself this "What does the Lord say?". Will he call you "Good and faithful servant" or an "evil coward". I know, that sounds harsh, but that's what the scripture says. Don't we all wish we could be making everyone happy with our words, but that is not our job? Our duty is to speak the truth in Love, snatching up those about to perish.

Biblical Examples of Why Some Fall Away

Envy

False Teachings

Temptation

Wickedness

Laziness

Fear, lack of faith, no fear of the Lord

Love of money

Standing with the wrong crowd

Unbelief

How can I help my fallen brother? Remind them that we must all repent of our sins

Revelations 2:5 Remember therefore from whence thou art fallen, and repent, and do the first works; or else I will come unto thee quickly, and will remove thy candlestick out of his place, except thou repent.

Teach them to listen carefully and cling tightly to the Good News: But you must continue to believe this truth and stand firmly in it. Don't fall away from the assurance you received when you heard the Good News. The Good News has been preached all over the world, and I, Paul, have been appointed as God's servant to proclaim it. So we must listen very carefully to the truth we have heard, or we may fall away from it.

Warn them of false teachings and doctrines:

2Thessalonions 2:3 Let no man deceive you by any means: for *that day shall not come,* except there come a falling away first, and that man of sin be revealed, the son of perdition;

Tell them they have to choose. Do you belong to the World or to the Lord? Warn them of the dangers of being lukewarm.

Luke 8:13 They on the rock *are they,* which, when they hear, receive the word with joy; and these have no root, which for a while believe, and in time of temptation fall away.

Continue to minister to them:

Colossians 1:23 If ye continue in the faith grounded and settled, and *be* not moved away from the hope of the gospel, which ye have heard, *and* which was preached to every creature which is under heaven; whereof I Paul am made a minister;

We need to start praying always for believers everywhere, without ceasing.

Tell the people: Tell them, as sure as I am the living God, I take no pleasure from the death of the wicked. I want the wicked to change their ways and live. Turn your life around! Reverse your evil ways! Why die, Israel?

Tell the people: There's more, son of man. Tell your people, a good person's good life won't save him when he decides to rebel and a bad person's bad life won't prevent him from repenting of his rebellion. A good person who sins can't expect to live when he chooses to sin. It's true that I tell good people, "Live! Be alive!" But if they trust in their good deeds and turn to evil, that good life won't amount to a hill of beans. They'll die for their evil life.

Tell the people: On the other hand, if I tell a wicked person, "You'll die for your wicked life," and he repents of his sin and starts living a righteous and just life—being generous to the down-and-out, restoring what he had stolen, cultivating life-nourishing ways that don't hurt others—he'll live. He won't die. None of his sins will be kept on the books. He's doing what's right, living a good life. He'll live. When good people turn back from living good lives and plunge into sin, they'll die for it. And when a wicked person turns away from his wicked life and starts living a just and righteous life, he'll come alive.

Do you ask yourself- Who am I?

Revelations 5:10 And hast made us unto our God kings and priests: and we shall reign on the earth.

1Peter 2:9 But ye *are* a chosen generation, a royal priesthood, an holy nation, a peculiar people; that ye should shew forth the praises of him who hath called you out of darkness into his marvellous light:

Revelations 1:6 And hath made us kings and priests unto God and his Father; to him *be* glory and dominion for ever and ever. Amen.

1Peter 2:5 Ye also, as lively stones, are built up a spiritual house, an holy priesthood, to offer up spiritual sacrifices, acceptable to God by Jesus Christ.

A gatekeeper protects the house of the Lord from corruption and worldly ideas. Stand true to the Word of God and do not waver. Protect the people from following lies, false ideas and wrong doctrine. Protect and cling tightly to the Word of God, protecting the Lord's house and His Ways. You must keep the people from stumbling off the narrow path. Keep the Lord's sheep safe until He comes back again, always staying ready and looking out for your master to return. He has commanded us to watch for His return.

Scriptures to Study:

Nehemiah 7:3 And I said unto them, Let not the gates of Jerusalem be opened until the sun be hot; and while they stand by, let them shut the doors, and bar *them:* and appoint watches of the inhabitants of Jerusalem, every one in his watch, and every one *to be* over against his house.

Nehemiah 10:39 For the children of Israel and the children of Levi shall bring the offering of the corn, of the new wine, and the oil, unto the chambers, where *are* the vessels of the sanctuary, and the priests that minister, and the porters, and the singers: and we will not forsake the house of our God.

Psalms 84:10 For a day in thy courts *is* better than a thousand. I had rather be a doorkeeper in the house of my God, than to dwell in the tents of wickedness.

Mark 13:34 *For the Son of man is* as a man taking a far journey, who left his house, and gave authority to his servants, and to every man his work, and commanded the porter to watch.

John 10:3 To him the porter openeth; and the sheep hear his voice: and he calleth his own sheep by name, and leadeth them out.

Colossians 1:23 If ye continue in the faith grounded and settled, and *be* not moved away from the hope of the gospel, which ye have heard, *and* which was preached to every creature which is under heaven; whereof I Paul am made a minister;

Hebrews 2:1 Therefore we ought to give the more earnest heed to the things which we have heard, lest at any time we should let *them* slip.

Psalms 141:4 Incline not my heart to *any* evil thing, to practise wicked works with men that work iniquity: and let me not eat of their dainties.

Psalms 18:36 Thou hast enlarged my steps under me, that my feet did not slip.

Job 12:5 He that is ready to slip with *his* feet *is as* a lamp despised in the thought of him that is at ease.

Hebrews 6:6 If they shall fall away, to renew them again unto repentance; seeing they crucify to themselves the Son of God afresh, and put *him* to an open shame.

2Thessalonions 2:3 Let no man deceive you by any means: for *that day shall not come,* except there come a falling away first, and that man of sin be revealed, the son of perdition;

Luke 8:13 They on the rock *are they,* which, when they hear, receive the word with joy; and these have no root, which for a while believe, and in time of temptation fall away.

Colossians 1:23 If ye continue in the faith grounded and settled, and *be* not moved away from the hope of the gospel, which ye have heard, *and* which was preached to every creature which is under heaven; whereof I Paul am made a minister;

Acts 20:24 But none of these things move me, neither count I my life dear unto myself, so that I might finish my course with joy, and the ministry, which I have received of the Lord Jesus, to testify the gospel of the grace of God.

Acts 17:5 But the Jews which believed not, moved with envy, took unto them certain lewd fellows of the baser sort, and gathered a company, and set all the city on an uproar, and assaulted the house of Jason, and sought to bring them out to the people.

Acts 2:25 For David speaketh concerning him, I foresaw the Lord always before my face, for he is on my right hand, that I should not be moved:

Jeremiah 25:16 And they shall drink, and be moved, and be mad, because of the sword that I will send among them.

Proverbs 12:3 A man shall not be established by wickedness: but the root of the righteous shall not be moved.

Psalms 121:3 He will not suffer thy foot to be moved: he

that keepeth thee will not slumber.

Psalms 112:6 Surely he shall not be moved for ever: the righteous shall be in everlasting remembrance.

Psalms 66:9 Which holdeth our soul in life, and suffereth not our feet to be moved.

Psalms 62:6 He only *is* my rock and my salvation: *he is* my defence; I shall not be moved.

Psalms 62:2 He only *is* my rock and my salvation; *he is* my defence; I shall not be greatly moved.

Psalms 46:5 God *is* in the midst of her; she shall not be moved: God shall help her, *and that* right early.

Psalms 30:6 And in my prosperity I said, I shall never be moved.

Psalms 16:8 I have set the LORD always before me: because *he is* at my right hand, I shall not be moved.

1Chronicles 17:9 Also I will ordain a place for my people Israel, and will plant them, and they shall dwell in their place, and shall be moved no more; neither shall the children of wickedness waste them any more, as at the beginning,

Jude 1:24 Now unto him that is able to keep you from falling, and to present *you* faultless before the presence of his glory with exceeding joy,

2Peter 1:10 Wherefore the rather, brethren, give diligence to make your calling and election sure: for if ye do these things, ye shall never fall:

James 5:12 But above all things, my brethren, swear not, neither by heaven, neither by the earth, neither by any other oath: but let your yea be yea; and *your* nay, nay; lest ye fall into condemnation.

James 1:2 My brethren, count it all joy when ye fall into divers temptations;

Hebrews 4:11 Let us labour therefore to enter into that rest, lest any man fall after the same example of unbelief.

Christians Attacking Christians

Today we have more Churches attacking Churches and Christians attacking Christians more than ever before. It all starts because they believe God is in the attacks. God is not in us attacking people and their reputations. I personally have a problem with things Church leaders have said and done. I'm not going to attack them though. If anything I will pray for those I disagree with. We attack Christians when we should be attacking false teachings and false Doctrines being released in this hour. We should be taking a stand today in America concerning the evil in the world.

Why are Christians attacking Christians? They blame the other side! There have been Ministers who have fallen because of sexual affairs, homosexuality and even taking money. It doesn't matter how they fell. They are still brothers and sisters in the Lord. All they have to do is repent and even God forgives them. The thing with the Body of Christ today, if one man falls they throw the whole thing out.

Todd Bentley

He may have tattoos from the top of his head to his feet and some of those tattoos are freaky looking. What I mean by that is they appear to be tattoos of things almost no

Christian would have on their body. God only knows his heart and I've been in his meetings and I've seen people get out of wheel chairs and miracles like I've never seen. The thing hear is he has tapped into something in the supernatural that most of the Church doesn't even know. The Church judges him because of his looks, his divorce and getting married to his former nanny. The only difference between him and the Church is that he has been open about it in public. You can judge him however you want to but instead you may need to pray for the truth not flesh discerning. God spoke to me that Todd Bentley looks normal compared to the new breed God is raising up. Pastors will be riding their Harley's in and getting off and preaching in their leather. We are going to have pierced, tattooed, blue haired, green haired and odd looking people preaching the Gospel. God will anoint who He wishes and He don't look at the outside, He looks on the inside. I've personally been around a lot of ministries and I know that God has given Todd some keys to the miraculous. God said most who hate Todd are jealous of his success. Todd may have made mistakes but God still causes many to be saved, healed and miracles unlike most Churches in the world. People need to get their focus off of judging men like Todd and look at the shape of America. Todd Bentley stepped down for a couple of years of Ministry do to the relationship with his current wife. He went to through a season of restoration where he even spoke publicly about everything. How many who judge can say they have healings and miracles in every service. The Church has tried to throw away everything that happened in Lakeland Florida because of Todd's fall. I was there on the Healing Team for weeks. What about the time the man who was in a wheel chair for twenty five years and he got up and walked healed. I prayed for a woman who had a medal rod in her back and she couldn't bend over. She was healed and testified of the medal rod being gone out of her body. I know that I was not operating in my mantle but under Todd's Ministry, miracles were easy. This is not the popular thing to say but we need to hear this.

Jim Baker

Everybody put down Jim Baker for years because of his fall. He did his time and he is back in ministry. He was in prison but the thing is who are we to judge. What many do not know is that he was considered the most hated man in America. At the same time Billy Graham was considered the most loved man in America. While Jim Baker was in jail Billy Graham visited him. This is the most loved man visiting the most hated man. Sounds like something Jesus would do.

Christians On Attack

If the Church wants to do something have prayer meetings and pray right. We are not to pray curses. People pray for ministries to fall just because they disagree with them. I have had people pray against me and my Ministry. They pray for all our finances to be lost and for my wife and me to break up. They pray for the gifts to dry up because they disagree with the decisions I have made. Those prayers are witchcraft and they are curses from the pit of hell. When people pray curses in Jesus Name it does not mean that God is backing them. We cannot curse people and expect God to back our words.

Before I go any further I have a Word of the Lord to release, "Shut your filthy mouth or I'll shut it for you." There is no love; it is just a blame game to feed the media industry. It is taking many away from the Lord as their focus becomes on the media and not in His Presence.

In the highest point of the Litchfield Revival I was blamed for everything. People said that they picked up their lives and moved to Litchfield for me. Well if they move there for me, then that was not for God. I received a lot of emails and letters saying, "people changed their lives and you walked away." If you were hearing from God then you would have heard that I was leaving soon. The Revival didn't fall apart until later after I left but according to many I'm the only reason it fell. We had healings, miracles, signs and wonders every night and after I left ....nothing.

Remember the child thing if you are pointing a finger at me there are three pointing back at you. I will watch news occasionally as world event materialize but it does not consume my day. Let us be honest, why are most watching world events in such a way? They are hoping Jesus returns tomorrow so He can whisk them away from their personal tribulation they are experiencing. But the reality is that this time that is given to us must be used to draw closer to Him instead of looking for signs to get out of your personal tribulations.

If the Government makes rules that you can't speak the truth of what the Bible says, we are to line up with God before we adjust to please all the political correct ways. Some in the Church have not preached the truth because of fears of rocking the boats. Even homosexuality has become a powerful subject that preachers are not preaching truths about. They are afraid of the discrimination laws. My Bible says homosexuality is an abomination from the pit of hell. There is nothing that is going to change that. The Government cannot tell me what to preach when it comes to the Bible. We live in the land of the free but the Church isn't standing up for their freedom of religion.

Christians attacking Christians are on the rise. This judgment is not of the Lord. I was notified of being added to a web site of false prophets. On the list were Smith Wigglesworth, Kathryn Kuhlman, John G. Lake, John Kilpatrick and even my name Bill Vincent. A whole list of men and women of God I think are some of the most powerful people of God. I thought praise God I've actually gotten somewhere. I got put on a list among good people. This list had not one person on there that I would agree was a false prophet. Most of the men and women of God who put these posts on the web could not walk a mile in most of these men and women shoes.

Children Exposure

God told me to add some things concerning what our children are exposed to. There are some things that the Church needs to stand against on behalf of children.

There are many things on Television today such as witchcraft and psychics. I've been to Disney World probably twelve times. I have seen a lot of change in Disney. They removed Michael Jackson because his alleged molestation cases. After removing Michael Jackson they put somebody like Britney Spears in. When Michael Jackson was in with Disney, he already was known as the man who grabbed his crotch while dancing on stage. That was fine for Disney. The thing is they are child oriented and attempt to appear moral but they are not by putting half dressed singers with a partying reputation like Britney Spears. The Disney Channel and Disney movies are full of witchcraft today. Parents today are going to get to a place of not allowing any witchcraft and psychic activity in them. There is too much of that stuff and they make it look like white witchcraft but this is also of the devil.

Leviticus 19:31 Regard not them that have familiar spirits, neither seek after wizards, to be defiled by them: I *am* the LORD your God.

Galatians 5:19-26 Now the works of the flesh are manifest, which are *these;* Adultery, fornication, uncleanness, lasciviousness, Idolatry, witchcraft, hatred, variance, emulations, wrath, strife, seditions, heresies, Envyings, murders, drunkenness, revellings, and such like: of the which I tell you before, as I have also told *you* in time past, that they which do such things shall not inherit the kingdom of God. But the fruit of the Spirit is love, joy, peace, longsuffering, gentleness, goodness, faith, Meekness, temperance: against such there is no law. And they that are Christ's have crucified the flesh with the affections and lusts. If we live in the Spirit, let us also walk in the Spirit. Let us not be desirous of vain glory, provoking one another, envying one another.

Deuteronomy 18:10-12 There shall not be found among you *any one* that maketh his son or his daughter to pass through the fire, *or* that useth divination, *or* an observer of times, or an enchanter, or a witch, Or a charmer, or a consulter with familiar spirits, or a wizard, or a necromancer. For all that do these things *are* an abomination unto the LORD: and because of these abominations the LORD thy God doth drive them out from before thee.

There is not one part of he demonic that is good. This is not popular to some children because they love these certain shows. Witchcraft and psychic abilities are all an abomination to God. This means God hates them. You preach the truth to children they will get to the place if they see these kinds of things they will change the channel without being told to. We have two children in our home both of them do this. They are ten and twelve and they are getting their own discernment. It's about preaching the truth to your children. Raise up the way a child shall go and they will not depart from it. Even something I watched when I was a child like the Smurfs (little blue guys) has potions, spells and magic. We have to draw the line somewhere if we want to protect the ears and eyes of children.

There is stuff like Harry Potter and there is nothing good in it. Witchcraft is witchcraft. There is even a book "Looking for God in Harry Potter" that is out there. No matter what there is nothing God likes about witchcraft. The only way Harry Potter can be God like is if he got saved at the end.

What I say this for is that the spirits of witchcraft, divination, sorcery, psychics and more are being released in our living rooms. We are opening our homes to this by allowing children to watch this stuff. It can even cause our children to tap into the demonic realm at first as play and then it becomes reality. You may say "oh I don't believe those spirits can come through the television." Let talk about PORN then. You would never let your children watch porn because it would affect them correct?

Video Games

We've got video games today that you rob someone's car. You can break open a car and take it. You might even shoot the person as you take their car. Many children have gotten tired of the fantasy of playing a game to doing the violence in real life. There is a lot of blood and gore in video games today. There is a thing put on games like MA which means for mature audience seventeen and older. The Body of Christ will even buy games with MA on the package where the children can decapitate people and blood gushes out of their neck and we wonder why children are angry sometimes. A lot of times parents try to be friends with their kids with no discipline. We need to realize most of the building of men and women started when they were children.

God said we have to be taking a stand where our children are concerned. Many children love the show called Dora. It seems like the most innocent show but then they start doing chants. Witchcraft is not always going to be just the demonic worshipers that are obvious witchcraft. The enemy comes through the innocent looking thing to penetrate our homes with the demonic realm. If the Church accepts the demonic then the whole world will. A former ministry friend had me in his home and his boy wanted to show me his new game. He was cutting people's heads off and stabbing others. There was blood all over the place. This boy was about seven years old. The ministry friend said before that his boy was having nightmares and all kinds of anger coming out. This game looked more realistic than some movies in Hollywood. I said to the minister that this was his boy's problem and the minister replied oh that is no big deal, there is nothing wrong with it.

We have to protect the innocent ears of the one's whom cannot protect themselves. When they turn eighteen they get to do what they want but we should really raise children with restrictions when it comes to the demonic realm. If you do this your children will grow and become discerning of both good and evil. Many parents don't talk to their children about uncomfortable things and then the children have to learn from their friends and school. By the time most children are age eleven they are hearing about sex in school from other children.

Children dressed

Today children are dressing more provocative than any time I've ever seen. The youth in America and across the world should dress like children. The Bible says to the female race "your body belongs to your husband." You need to understand this means that even to the husband you will have later in life. No female should show revealing of any kind except for their husband. Unless females are in a pool they should have their clothes on. The reason for of all this is that we need to watch on behalf of our children because there are too many sick-people out there today. They prey and look at young girls like an adult because of the perverse mindsets they have. We've got to cover our children. When God said to add this topic; He said one of the biggest hits on the web today is seventeen and younger porn. I didn't research this because I knew there was going to be too much out there. Child porn is illegal but the internet has a license to kill. One thing is that the porn producers are feeding this sick child porn to potential molesters. I'm sure that some are just dressed to look young to arouse this lustful spirit. The freedoms in the world have gotten dangerous. The chat rooms can have a forty five year old man pretending to be a young boy or girl to draw children. The Church allows their children to be on facebook and even facebook requires the age to be thirteen and older. I know parents that sign them up on facebook anywhere from six to twelve years old. The thing is most do not set the security settings and they give children full access unsupervised. One child that got set-up a facebook account and when we looked into it she has a couple dozen older men on this nine to ten year old girls account.

Within a moment a child can be hurt or mad at their parents can be caroused by some man who acts like a child. They may offer them the world and even buy them things. Why do you think we have to keep telling our young children not to take candy from strangers? The problem is there are too many people that are out there full of devils. We need to realize that right under our nose there needs to be supervision.

Sound the Alarm is what this is about. God said to speak concerning all of this.

I believe any child that has a computer should have it in the living room. You may ask why? If they have passwords on anything the parents should have access. You may call it spying but I believe God calls it parenting.

Children today especially girl's ages eleven to seventeen are showing more than ever. They are showing cleavage, dressed in short-shorts, shorter skirts and low jeans. The world we live in has even caused the young undeveloped to stuff their bras with socks. It's bad enough anyone is like this but these are children. Someone's eyes will look and see through eyes of lust for a child. Children do not dress this way unless they have been exposed to it. They may be exposed through TV, friends and even parents.

We are supposed to be our children's role models. God said to me once that if the Church people didn't buy the skimpy clothes they would go out of business. People can say well they look so cute but the beauty is not about skin.

No More Delays

God is speaking that this is a year of swiftness, which means there are going to be no delays. Some of you have found delay after delay. Maybe it's your fault; maybe it's not. There's going to be no more delay; there's going to be a swift move of the Spirit!

There is a rise within the Church of Leviathan,

Python, and Jezebel and the hold are on many religious leaders. What is God saying now and let us realize that the spirit of pythos and the spirit of Jezebel have now sought each other so they could co-exist and they could become multiple powers. What does that mean for us? It means control, control, control. What happens first; they kill the prophets and suffocate a move of God. Control is not always bad but it's getting worse. This is dangerous when these souls try and co-exist, when there is evil and bad in the human soul, because the mischief doubles. The mischief multiplies as they co-exist. Jezebel worshipped Baal and surrounded herself with false prophets. She wanted Baal to have equal rights with Yahweh, the God of Israel. The God of the United States is Jesus Christ; no other is Lord. Jezebel's stance brought her into conflict with the prophet Elijah.

The reason that God is raising up prophets all over the world is because this spirit is so prevalent. This spirit is endeavoring to raise the names of religions and gods and make them equal with Christ; then it will get worse. Now we come to the real issue. A battle between Yahweh and Baal is about to take place in the United States of America *Jezebel, false prophets and python Spirits.* I want you to know that his force is bringing a conflict with the prophets because it has decided that it will dwell in the United States of America. The Spirit of Elijah that is coming upon the earth, like we have never seen before.

A sound like we have never heard before; I have never heard. I hope I live to see it, but there is something beyond this veil – a way that we could never imagine. I pray, Lord, that each Warrior would receive just a glimpse of this future; that You will rain upon land, upon land, upon land – upon schools, colleges. Let the church emerge, that we know about, that is in existence. Now, you pray for Israel, for you see, Warriors of God, it's not just Israel they want – they want you, America.

We stand as watchmen on the wall and declare, "So far and no more! I can change leaders; I can turn men from darkness to light. I can change their minds, and I shall," says the Lord. Watch how I shine upon this nation and in the presence of your enemies. Do not give up. God is with you, Israel, and God is with you, America and everyone in this place and everyone all over the world. I want you to understand that these things may look to you like, "My God, everything's coming to an end." What is God saying? What is God saying to us? Why are we so weak? Why are we so weak that we can fall to pieces when bad things happen? And I won't stop saying this: the greatest is yet to come. That which has never ever happened before – listen to me – is about to happen.

A lot of you are responding out of fear. Attention to the Churches that prey on the fears of people. I don't have fear because I have seen the other side. There may be a demon that may greet me when I get to the other side and there may have been a storm as I went to the other side, but what happened to the demoniac?

Jesus, in one hour, was able to free the man from legions of demons and change the economy of that entire city within one hour. How did He do that? (Goes on to preach about the power of Jesus to change things – even as people questioned Him. Speaking to the storm, etc.) There is a storm; God has been silent for a while. He comes forth and does wonderful things for us personally, but on a national scale, it seems like He's not doing anything and so people are crying out against the terrible crimes and sins which we agree with.

We disagree with abortion – we hate it; it's a crime, it's a sin – but just because that's happening does it mean that God is not able to intervene? Where is the faith? This is what Jesus said when He came out of that boat. He said, "Little faith! Do you not believe?" In other words, He was questioning them saying, "Lord, do you not care that we are perishing?" Maybe thousands of you, or millions, are saying, "Do You not care what is happening in America? Do You not care what is happening in the Middle of the greatest darkness covering the earth." God is about to show us the Church breakthrough.

Abortion Revealed

I'm going to lay a foundation of information concerning this subject of abortion. First we must look at facts.

Abortion is happening at a rapid rate.

What is abortion: A vacuum aspiration abortion at eight weeks gestational age (six weeks after fertilization)? Approximately 205 million pregnancies occur each year worldwide. Over a third are unintended and about a fifth end in induced abortion. Most abortions result from unintended pregnancies. A pregnancy can be intentionally aborted in several ways. The manner selected often depends upon the stage of the embryo or fetus, which increases in size as the pregnancy progresses. Specific procedures may also be selected due to legality, regional availability, and doctor or patient preference. Up to 15 weeks' gestation, suction-aspiration or vacuum aspiration is the most common surgical methods of induced abortion. *Manual vacuum aspiration* (MVA) consists of removing the fetus or embryo, placenta, and membranes by suction using a manual syringe, while *electric vacuum aspiration* (EVA) uses an electric pump.

God told me that babies are still being aborted at 36 weeks. It is illegal but America has opened the door and now they do this beyond the law. The speed limits many times are set as limits but that just causes people to go beyond the limit. The same goes for abortion.

If someone shoots a pregnant woman to a certain term they can be tried for a double murder. The law protects rights of life in one area called murder of the baby in the womb but not in the abortion of the baby.

From the 15th week of gestation until approximately the 26th, other techniques must be used. IDX is sometimes called "partial-birth abortion," which has been federally banned in the United States.

Generally, the former position argues that a human fetus is a human being with a right to live, making abortion morally the same as murder. The latter position argues that a woman has certain reproductive rights, especially the choice whether or not to carry a pregnancy to term.

They have the right to choose. Well they have the right to choose to have sex so maybe that ought to be stopped if they have an abortion.

Sex-selective abortion

Sonography and amniocentesis allow parents to determine sex before childbirth. The development of this technology has led to sex-selective abortion, or the termination of a fetus based on sex (male and female). The selective termination of a female fetus is most common.

How many times are there a false reading of a sonogram and they abort because it's not what they wanted or a possible defect. If the reading in false it doesn't matter.

Sex-selective abortion is partially responsible for the noticeable disparities between the birth rates of male and female children in some countries. The preference for male children is reported in many areas of Asia, and abortion used to limit female births has been reported in Taiwan, South Korea, India, and China. This also happens in America.

No one should be able to get pregnant and then abort because there is or isn't a penis.

This deviation from the standard birth rates of males and females occurs despite the fact that the country in question may have officially banned sex-selective abortion or even sex-screening.

The following quotations are taken directly from medical and psychological studies on teen abortions. About 20 per cent of all abortions taking place in the U.S. today are performed on teens. Teenage abortion has been linked to a number of physical and psychological problems, including drug and alcohol abuse, suicide attempts and suicidal ideation, and other self-destructive behaviors. The number and types of physical complications resulting from abortion are as diverse as the various abortion methods. Depending upon the type of abortion performed, physical complications can be as follows:

- Cervical tearing and laceration from the instruments. Perforation of the uterus by instruments. This may require major surgery, including hysterectomy. Scarring of the uterine lining by suction tubing,

- Infection, local and systemic.
- Hemorrhage and shock, especially if the uterine artery is torn.
- Anesthesia toxicity from both general or local anesthesia, resulting in possible convulsions, cardio-respiratory arrest, and in extreme cases, death.
- Retained tissue, indicated by cramping, heavy bleeding, and infection. An enlarged, tender and soft uterus retaining blood clots.
- Failure to recognize an ectopic pregnancy. This could lead to the rupture of a fallopian tube, hemorrhage, and resulting infertility or death, if treatment is not provided in time.

Listen Church we preach the Word of God but we shy away from truths such as abortion and it's affects on America's people.

Some women experience immediate psychological problems from abortion. Other women repress feelings of guilt, delaying emotional reactions sometimes for several years and oftentimes triggered by their first planned pregnancy.

These complications include:

Sad mood

Sudden and uncontrollable crying episodes

Deterioration of self-concept

Sleep, appetite and sexual disturbances

Reduced motivation

Disruption in interpersonal relationships

Extreme guilt and anxiety

Psychological "numbing"

Depression and thoughts of suicide

It's easy for a young man to ask his teenage girl friend to abort their baby so it doesn't hinder his future. The females of this world are chronically affected by this procedure. Men can continue their sexual egg hunts with no effects.

Many Christians have had abortions. The reason being is because the Church doesn't look beyond the surface of this. China kills babies freely but America is supposed to be the land of the free. Babies are desired by many through adoption. We need to ask God to have mercy on America for abortions while the Church sleeps. What happens to created aborted babies? They are thrown away in the garbage.

We need to pray, write to our political leaders, preach about these type of subjects and take a stand as a Church.

Morning After Pill

This is a time we must hear what God has to say to the Church. God is giving us prayer strategies like never before. Things we are talking about in this book are the very causes of the hindrances in the Church all across the world. This is to open the eyes of the Church to realize there is much more going on in America than we all know about.

Everything science discovers at first seems to be a good thing. I'm going to list a lot of facts for us to look at what America calls The Morning After Pill and I call The Abortion Pill.

What happens, when a pill is created and women or even young girls can have sex and then take a pill after and it will not allow the pregnancy? This gives young women a legal gun in their hands.

The German Catholic church allows morning-after pill in rape cases.

The emergency contraceptive/morning-after pill has three modes of action (as does the regular birth control pill); that is, it can work in one of three ways:

- The normal menstrual cycle is altered, delaying ovulation; or

- Ovulation is inhibited, meaning the egg will not be released from the ovary;
- It can irritate the lining of the uterus so as to inhibit implantation.

The beginning of birth: The newly **created child** then travels down the fallopian tube to the uterus (womb) where he or she implants. Implantation is necessary for the new child to receive nourishment from the mother and continue developing. The journey from the fallopian tube to the womb takes between five and seven days during which pregnancy cannot be readily detected.

Therefore, if a woman ingests emergency contraception after fertilization has taken place, the third mode of action can occur. The lining of the uterus can be altered causing the woman's body to reject the living human embryo, making implantation impossible and the child will die. This result is called a chemical abortion; therefore emergency contraception is an abortifacient.

Two of the most commonly used emergency contraceptive pills are Preven and Plan B. The websites for both of these drugs clearly indicate that each can work to prevent a "fertilized egg" (which is actually a newly formed human being) from implanting in the uterine wall: "emergency contraception," as well as the Preven and Plan B websites, contend that emergency contraception does not cause abortion.

If you take away the nutrients required the seed cannot live.

They argue that emergency contraception prevents pregnancy and thereby reduces the need for induced abortion. However, they intentionally define the term "pregnancy" as implantation of a fertilized egg in the lining of a woman's uterus, as opposed to "pregnancy" beginning at fertilization.

(POLITICALLY CORRECT)

Whether one understands pregnancy as beginning at "implantation" or "fertilization," the heart of the matter is when human life begins. It is important to keep in mind that scientists have confirmed that at the moment the sperm and the egg join (fertilization), a new human being is created who is completely different from his/her mother. This is not a subjective opinion, but an objective scientific fact.

A San Francisco - Girl went to a Planned Parenthood clinic to quietly consider ways to handle a life change she wasn't ready for. One week later, the 18-year-old lay dying on an emergency room table, the victim of complications after she took the abortion pill. Her death has already caused her grief-stricken father to hope that the tragedy will encourage other women considering abortion to seek support, especially from their families. She visited a Planned Parenthood clinic September 10th to take the pill. She followed the prescribed procedure for using RU-486, taking two more pills at home in the following days. After experiencing bleeding and cramps so severe that she was unable to walk, her boyfriend rushed her to the hospital, where she was given painkillers and sent home. She was back in the hospital a few days later and died September 17th. Her dad said he learned from an attending physician at the hospital that she had died after a massive infection caused by ***fragments of the fetus left inside her uterus caused her to go into septic shock****.*

Someone sexually active doesn't really know for sure whether or not they are pregnant. What I mean is they may have had sex for weeks and used a defective condom. They became pregnant and then weeks later they have sex with sure knowledge the sperm sent into them so now they go to get the Morning After Pill. Taking this pill while already pregnant can cause a lot of problems or even death. In Indiana they are passing a law that says if you want to use the Morning After Pill you must have an Ultrasound or Sonogram to see if you are already pregnant. A new baby seeking nutrients from the mother is in some ways starved by the mother.

All this pill does is give teens and young women the freedom to have sex without consequences. See the thing is they are more concerned about having a baby then the STD (Sexually Transmitted Disease) that is possible through sex. After being raped is one thing but then it opens the door to more use. Many times all the drug companies see is dollar signs. The safe guards that are in place are not enough if someone dies or babies are aborted in taking this pill.

In Vitro Fertilization

I will list some of the facts again so we can get a full grasp on what God has put His finger on this for.

IVF may be used to overcome female infertility in the woman due to problems of the fallopian tube, making fertilization *in vivo* difficult. It may also assist in male infertility, where there is a defect in sperm quality, and in such cases intracytoplasmic sperm injection (ICSI) may be used, where a sperm cell is injected directly into the egg cell. This is used when sperm have difficulty penetrating the egg, and in these cases the partner's or a donor's sperm may be used. IVF can also be used with egg donation or surrogacy where the woman providing the egg isn't the same who will carry the pregnancy to term.

Birth defects

In 2008, an analysis of the data of the National Birth Defects Study in the US found that certain birth defects were significantly more common in infants conceived through IVF, notably septal heart defects, cleft lip with or without cleft palate, esophageal atresia, and anorectal atresia; the mechanism of causality is unclear.

Leftover embryos or eggs

There may be leftover embryos or eggs from IVF procedures if the woman for whom they were originally created has successfully carried one or more pregnancies to term. These may be donated to help other women or couples as a means of third party reproduction. In embryo donation, these extra embryos are given to other couples or women for transfer with the goal of producing a successful pregnancy. The resulting child is considered the child of the woman who carries it and gives birth, and not the child of the donor, the same occurs with egg donation or sperm donation. Some people believe donation of leftover embryos for research is a good alternative to discarding the embryos when patients receive proper, honest and clear information about the research project, the procedures and the scientific values.

Remember that God considered life at fertilization stage.

Same-sex Couples, Unmarried Parents

Two lesbian women walk into a clinic and one walks out pregnant …. You cannot tell me hat God is in favor of that. Homosexuality is an abomination to God. All babies are created by God!

A single woman can go and have a baby. It is supposed to be a Husband and Wife according to scriptures that have babies.

A 2009 statement from the ASRM found no persuasive evidence that children are harmed or disadvantaged solely by being raised by single parents, unmarried parents, or homosexual parents. It did not support restricting access to assisted reproductive technologies on the basis of a prospective parent's marital status or sexual orientation. Adoption has more rules than sperm donation. Ethical concerns include reproductive rights, the welfare of offspring, nondiscrimination against unmarried individuals, homosexual, and professional autonomy. A recent controversy in California focused on the question of whether physicians opposed to same-sex relationships should be required to perform IVF for a lesbian couple.

A new baby will be able to be born into homes of lesbians (women partners), single parents with no dad or even gay (men partners with a segregate).

Christians don't think about all of this because we only see the surface. When is enough enough.

When they receive the donor's sperm they don't really know the facts of the person. They just know what they put on paper and their sample in a jar. They have no knowledge of the real psychological, demonic or even the true history of this man. An aids test is not enough information about donors. We have enough trouble in the Church dealing with generational curses, genetic backgrounds and we could even get to the point that you couldn't know if it was your own blood line the sperm was donated from. Your brother could have donated and you received his sample. There are some testing procedures in place but over all this is scientific pregnancy at its best.

What about a demon possessed man who goes to donate sperm?

After going through deliverance with hundreds of people I learned something powerful. This is especially in the realm of lust and perversion. God has shown me that many times these spirits come during time of conception. The man or women allows fantasy, imagination, or even multiple partners during conception. That baby has been released a seed of lust and perversion from the mother's womb. It's called transference of spirits. This also happens when the donor's masturbating into a cup for a sample of sperm. Most of these places have room full of porn to stimulate the erection. If you are having sex with your husband or wife and you imagine someone else you have committed adultery in your own heart.

Mat 5:28 But I say unto you, That whosoever looketh on a woman to lust after her hath committed adultery with her already in his heart.

I personally cast out over a thousand demons out of a woman and the root that had to be broke was; when she was conceived her mother was part of an orgy and got pregnant. This caused massive open doors to the spirits of lust.

Anonymous donors

Some children conceived by IVF using anonymous donors report being troubled over not knowing about their donor parent as well any genetic relatives they may have and their family history.

In the U.K., Sweden, Norway, Germany, Italy, New Zealand, and some Australian states, donors aren't paid and can't be anonymous.

Single people seeking to get pregnant

I knew a guy when I was in the world that needed drug money and he would get dressed up and go to many places to sell his sperm. He was a demonic drug addict.

You could receive sperm from siblings, family without any knowledge, Serial killers, homosexual, generational cursed people.

Science has confirmed that there is something wrong in the DNA of serial killers but yet they could donate sperm. The person donating could be homosexual and those spirits could be passed on.

The reason why I'm talking about this is because America is on the verge of something evil. The next step is cloning of people. Some can clone people for spare parts. This is not a sci-fi movie. God told me years ago that it wouldn't be long before I would be able to look at a person and not be able to prophesy to them. The reason being is they will be soulless. If science can create a baby in a tray how much farther is it to create a person. God is speaking that science is trying to become God and this is by creating by breaking laws of the spirit. There are always underground hidden scientists going against the restrictions for scientific breakthroughs.

God talks about seeds all through the Bible don't you think He knew about this and there is revelations in it.

Catholic objections

The Roman Catholic Church opposes all kinds of *in vitro* fertilization because, as with contraception, it separates the procreative purpose of the marriage act from its purpose: The reason is that the fundamental nature of the marriage act, while uniting husband and wife in the closest intimacy, also renders them capable of generating new life—and this as a result of laws written into the actual nature of man and of woman.

To up the odds of success they will even plant 2-3 seeds to get a woman pregnant. If they succeed to get the desired percentage change of a boy or girl they will terminate the rest. Abortion again is connected to this. What about the tray of left unused eggs may be discarded or given to another woman. Wow!

We need to pray to break curses off of anyone whom has already used this procedure. The Church needs to speak up. This is a dangerous thing because it has too many possibilities.

Homosexuality

I'm going to list a lot of facts to give us the full picture of Homosexuality.

Legality of Sodomy law is even in the prisons in America. But yet we in America are gradually allowing same sex marriage. This is really messed up where the Church is today. We don't want to offend the homosexuals. First of all a man that has sex with a man and a woman that has sex with a woman is an abomination to God. This means that God hates it. I want to give attention to every Pastor, Leader and Minister whom put together a same sex marriage should step down from ministry in my opinion. They are living a life as a hypocrite by agreeing with this world that homosexuality is okay. It goes against the very Word of God. If the government tries to force me to perform a same sex marriage, I will go to jail first. I'm not going to adjust my beliefs just because of this discrimination act that is being established right now.

I don't agree with hate crimes. I don't believe in stoning, killing or attacking someone because they are homosexual it is wrong. We have to realize that we are not dealing with the person but principalities, powers and rulers in high places.

They are not born homosexual like some believe. It comes

from other spirits and curses that cause bad decisions of homosexual tendencies.

Abraham said that all men are created equal but this spirit is not part of that. I have seen deliverance of many whom have sexual desires of multiple woman or men all swapping sexual pleasures. You cannot tell me that is normal.

Most nations do not prohibit consensual sex between unrelated persons above the local age of consent. Some jurisdictions further recognize identical rights, protections, and privileges for the family structures of same-sex couples, including marriage.

Some nations mandate that all individuals restrict themselves to heterosexual relationships; that is, in some jurisdictions homosexual activity is illegal. Offenders can face the death penalty in some fundamentalist Muslim areas such as Iran and parts of Nigeria.

On the other hand, many countries today in the Middle East and Africa, as well as several countries in Asia, the Caribbean and the South Pacific, outlaw homosexuality. In six countries, homosexual behavior is punishable by life imprisonment; in ten others, it carries the death penalty.

Laws against sexual orientation discrimination

United States

Employment discrimination refers to discriminatory employment practices such as bias in hiring, promotion, job assignment, termination, and compensation, and various types of harassment. In the United States there is "very little statutory, common law, and case law establishing employment discrimination based upon sexual orientation as a legal wrong." Some exceptions and alternative legal strategies are available.

According to some laws a Church would have to hire a homosexual person if they apply for a job. It's not about qualifications but I don't want the spirits involved with Church things. They need God just like all sinners.

President Bill Clinton's Executive Order 13087 (1998) prohibits discrimination based on sexual orientation in the competitive service of the federal civilian workforce, and federal non-civil service employees may have recourse under the due process clause of the U.S. Constitution.

Housing discrimination refers to discrimination against potential or current tenants by landlords.

It is like over night homosexual's have more rights.

In the United States, there is no federal law against such discrimination on the basis of sexual orientation or gender identity, but at least thirteen states and many major cities have enacted laws prohibiting it.

Hate crimes (also known as **bias crimes**) are crimes motivated by bias against an identifiable social group, usually groups defined by race (classification of human beings), religion, sexual orientation, disability, ethnicity, nationality, age, gender, gender identity, or political affiliation.

It should be a crime to attack someone for being homosexual.

Military service

The US Army defines homosexual conduct as "a homosexual act, a statement by a soldier that demonstrates a propensity or intent to engage in homosexual acts, the solicitation of another to engage in homosexual act or acts, or a homosexual marriage or attempted marriage."

Some countries allow gay men, lesbians, and bisexual people to serve openly and have granted them the same rights and privileges as their heterosexual counterparts. The other two generally do not: China bans gay and lesbian people outright; Russia excludes all gay and lesbian people during peacetime but allows some gay men to serve in wartime (see below). Israel is the only country in the Middle East region that allows openly people to serve in the military.

While the question of homosexuality in the military has been highly politicized in the United States, it is not necessarily so in many countries. Generally speaking, sexuality in these cultures is considered a more personal aspect of one's identity than it is in the United States.

On March 18, 2010, after U.S. President Obama announced that he wanted to put an end to the Don't Ask, Don't Tell policy, former U.S. general and high ranking

NATO official blamed homosexuals serving in the Dutch military for the fall of Srebrenica to Serb militias in the Bosnian War fifteen years earlier, stating that homosexuals had weakened the Dutch UN battalion charged with protecting the commune.

Religion

Though the relationship between homosexuality and religion can vary greatly across time and place, within and between different religions and sects, and regarding different forms of homosexuality and bisexuality, current authoritative bodies and doctrines of the world's largest religions generally view homosexuality negatively. This can range from quietly discouraging homosexual activity, to explicitly forbidding same-sex sexual practices among adherents and actively opposing social acceptance of homosexuality. Some teach that homosexual orientation itself is sinful, others state that only the sexual act is a sin, others are completely accepting of gays and lesbians, while some encourage homosexuality. Some claim that homosexuality can be overcome through religious faith and practice. On the other hand, voices exist within many of these religions that view homosexuality more positively, and liberal religious denominations may bless same-sex marriages.

The Church needs to get back to the truths of scripture. We cannot change the Word of God.

Homosexual's are on most shows on TV than ever before.

It is kind of like when Madonna and Britney Spears kissed. Two of the most powerful seducing women of their generation coming together.

Leviticus 20:13 If a man also lie with mankind, as he lieth with a woman, both of them have committed an abomination: they shall surely be put to death; their blood *shall be* upon them.

Leviticus 18:22-24 Thou shalt not lie with mankind, as with womankind: it *is* abomination. Neither shalt thou lie with any beast to defile thyself therewith: neither shall any woman stand before a beast to lie down thereto: it *is* confusion. Defile not ye yourselves in any of these things: for in all these the nations are defiled which I cast out before you:

Jude testifies about God's fiery destruction of Sodom for "sexual immorality": (SODOMY)

Jude 1:7 Even as Sodom and Gomorrha, and the cities about them in like manner, giving themselves over to fornication, and going after strange flesh, are set forth for an example, suffering the vengeance of eternal fire.

Exactly what type of "sexual immorality" and "strange flesh" had the Sodomites "gone after"? It was homosexuality:

Genesis 19:4, 5 But before they lay down, the men of the city, *even* the men of Sodom, compassed the house round, both old and young, all the people from every quarter: And they called unto Lot, and said unto him, Where *are* the men which came in to thee this night? bring them out unto us, that we may know them.

President Barack Obama

I'm not going after the President. I'm just releasing things that come straight out of his mouth. I have already mentioned Bill Clinton, Barack Obama and the first ladies in my book "Rapture Revelations." A lot of what I have mentioned in this book has been since these men have taken office.

I may have said this before but the cover of this book is America on fire. More and more bad decisions are being made by our leaders political and spiritual. These decisions are causing an opening of many doors of hell right here on earth. We are losing our freedom of religion while the demonic freedom of abortion and same sex marriage are running with more freedom.

There will be a day where the world will have to get the mark of the beast (666) to eat or enjoy any freedoms at all. This is satan's mark and it is my belief (according to scripture) that once anyone receives this mark will not be saved.

Obama's Beliefs,

While President Barack Obama's beliefs today are claimed to be Christian beliefs, what he shared candidly about his beliefs prior to setting his sights on the presidency warrants a closer look.

Discussed hereafter are Barack Obama's beliefs as he shared them in a rare 2004 interview with Chicago Sun-Times, as well as the then candidate Barack Obama's January 2008 revelation about his beliefs. Barack Obama responds to the more pinpointed questions below about his beliefs. In his April 2004 interview, Barack Obama expounded: "The difficult thing about any religion, including Christianity, is that at some level there is a call to evangelize and proselytize. There's the belief, certainly in some quarters, that if people haven't embraced Jesus Christ as their personal savior, they're going to hell."

Instead, Barack Obama stated:

"What I believe in is that if I live my life as well as I can, that I will be rewarded. I don't presume to have knowledge of what happens after I die." *(Barack Obama, April 2004)* "I believe that there are many paths to the same place, and that is a belief that there is a higher power, a belief that we are connected as a people, that there are values that transcend race or culture, that move us forward, and that there's an obligation for all of us individually as well as collectively to take responsibility to make those values lived." *(Barack Obama, April 2004)*

Note also that the "paths" in Barack Obama's Christianity leads not to a person but a "place", and not to "the Father" but a "higher power".

It was proven before he was President that he did not visit his Church frequently. All candidates do this for a good image. It's not Republican or Democrat any more. I consider three major issues when voting; freedom of religion, same sex marriage and abortion. These are the things important to God so they are important to me. President Obama has danced around these important issues but he has admittedly supported abortion, same sex marriage and even made decisions against freedom of religion. Muslims he has supported openly though.

God's has promised there will be a woman in the White House. A woman will be a big help to America as President according to God.

Prayer in School

I want to talk about one of the greatest failures in our Nation. When the government removed prayer from school things began to change. The violence in schools has been on an all time high. Now many schools have metal detectors to stop students from bringing knives and guns to school. Even in Litchfield they have added an entrance monitor that you have to buzz your way in.

United States

In the United States, public schools are banned from conducting religious observances such as prayer. The legal basis for this prohibition is the First Amendment to the United States Constitution, which requires that Congress shall make no law respecting an establishment of religion, or prohibiting the free exercise thereof...

Arguments for and against school prayer

The issue of school prayer remains contentious even where courts as diverse as those in Canada, the United States, Russia, and Poland attempt to strike a balance between religious and secular activity in state-sponsored arenas. In recent years, programs derived from **yoga**, a **Hindu** religious practice, have been introduced into public schools in the U.S. Advocates for the programs say they help children to relax and concentrate, but critics counter that the programs violate the separation of church and state.

If the school practices any of the false religions you can contact the school and have your children not to take part because of religious beliefs.

We were allowed to pray in school when I was a child and then we had a moment of silence. Now most schools don't have anything.

The argument is that we can't have prayer in school they don't want religious beliefs shoved down their throat. I don't want my children to be exposed to the world being created from a Big Bang Theory or that we all come from apes. They teach these things as fact but nothing concerning Adam and Even in the beginning.

We need to take a stand and establish some kind of prayer for children off of school grounds to try to start media frenzy or something to wake up the Body of Christ before it is too late.

We spend all the money on sports but no attention to prayer in school. Wake up Church.

God's Freedoms

In Hillsboro, IL, where we used to have a Church some anti-God men fought to get "In God We Trust" off of the Court House. After a long fight they won. They were stating that there had to be a separation of religion and justice. What they didn't know is a main Church within the back of their building facing the main highway bought the sign. Today it hangs and even lights up for every person who enters the City to see it.

Our Nation was established as In God We Trust and slowly God is being removed from our Nation. The Church and America are sitting by while people are fighting to remove God.

They are also trying to get God off of money. Even the new Dollar coin only has it printed on the edge and after it's in circulation for a short time it fades off. They have talked about a one world currency and when something like that happens "In God We Trust" won't be on that money.

There is preaching about finding God in any religion. Jesus is the only way. Jesus says, I'm the way the truth and the life no man cometh to the Father but by Me. Jesus is the only way to God.

We have to stop trying to be politically correct. You are either in or out. You can preach out of both sides of your mouth. We cannot pet demons in people. You can't rub the tummy of a budda stature to get to heaven folks. Preachers need to start opening their mouth about our freedoms and shut their mouths concerning being the critic of the Church.

Freedom of Religion has been slipping away. America is always banning a religion in work places. We are not allowed in many places to talk about our faith. Muslims have been given more rights since Obama has took office and we have lost more where Christianity is concerned. There is a tighter ban on what preachers can say political views, homosexuality and more. The goal here is if a Church has the 501C-3 and preaches the truth of homosexuality they can be shut down or even arrested by the government. Freedom of religion is slipping away and we need to rise together and pray.

What About Yoga?

I want to talk about one of the most popular exercises today in the world. I'm going to list facts so I can respond with truth of what God is saying.

Yoga

Religious ties not exercise. Connected to hindu, buddists, islam, musslims and many false religions.

Christian meditation

Some Christians integrate yoga and other aspects of Eastern spirituality with prayer and meditation. This has been attributed to a desire to experience God in a more complete way.

The Roman Catholic Church and some other Christian organizations have expressed concerns and disapproval with respect to some eastern and New Age practices that include yoga and meditation.

Question: ***"What is the Christian view of yoga?"***

Answer: For many Christians in the West who don't understand the history behind it, yoga is simply a means of physical exercise and strengthening and improving flexibility of the muscles. However, the philosophy behind yoga is much more than physically improving oneself. It is an ancient practice derived from India, believed to be the path to spiritual growth and enlightenment. The word *yoga* means "union," and the goal is to unite one's transitory (temporary) self with the infinite Brahman, the Hindu concept of "God."

You become one with yourself which removed the one true God and opens the door to false gods. What about the DVD's you may own. BURN THEM. I'm not going to mince any words about it. Yoga is from the demonic realm. Hatha yoga is the aspect of yoga which focuses on the physical body through special postures, breathing exercises, and concentration or meditation. The practice of yoga is based on the belief that man and God are one. It is little more than self-worship disguised as high-level spirituality. You get to a place you worship yourself and the reason you feel better is because of the demonic energy.

The question becomes, is it possible for a Christian to isolate the physical aspects of yoga as simply a method of exercise, without incorporating the spirituality or philosophy behind it? Yoga originated with a blatantly anti-Christian philosophy, and that philosophy has not changed.

The Church opens them to this cult like activity. Many medical logos have a yoga position right in them. It teaches one to focus on oneself instead of on the one true God. It encourages its participants to seek the answers to life's difficult questions within their own conscience instead of in the Word of God. It also leaves one open to deception from God's enemy, who searches for victims that he can turn away from God

I had a woman come to my Church who said she was trained in deliverance and I had a lot of people needing set free. I thought I'll give it a shot but I wanted her to record the session. I listened to it and she kept saying find your inner Porpoise go after your inner Porpoise and I was blown away. The entire session had nothing about Jesus, the blood or even the Holy Spirit. I asked her if she still had a manual of this deliverance training she went through. On the cover was someone posed in yoga like state? I had to spend a couple hours to undo what that so called deliverance had done. What's Porpoise got to do with deliverance?

1Peter 5:8 Be sober, be vigilant; because your adversary the devil, as a roaring lion, walketh about, seeking whom he may devour:

1Corinthians 10:31 Whether therefore ye eat, or drink, or whatsoever ye do, do all to the glory of God.

Philippians 4:8 Finally, brethren, whatsoever things are true, whatsoever things *are* honest, whatsoever things *are* just, whatsoever things *are* pure, whatsoever things *are* lovely, whatsoever things *are* of good report; if *there be* any virtue, and if *there be* any praise, think on these things.

Yoga can open up to spirits that can expose you to the demonic realm. Even today's game Wii has yoga in the work out part of the game. Remember God said these were things He wanted to Sound the Alarm about.

Wake Up Call

Obama has been a wake up call to the coming Anti-Christ. Here is what I mean by that. He has been called the coming Messiah; he's been called the savior to America. He has been worshiped and he has not rejected in any way these high praises only worthy of Jesus. The Anti-Christ is going to sneak right in and the world will receive him well. Obama had most of the kinds of things happening during his campaign that most would never have received. America slept especially the Church and lifted him up to a place worthy of no man.

The Church must rise with its back bone intact. In other words stop petting demons. If a leader is not going to preach the truth then he needs to shut his mouth. We have to call sin is sin and repent for the Kingdom of God is at hand. If a preacher does not preach the truth and people go to hell then their blood is on the hands of the preacher. I would rather not be popular and preach the truth then to be popular.

Pastors and leaders must unite and take the role that God has given them. Leaders need to stop talking bad about ministers and come together in unity. It is time to tear down denominational walls for the saving of America before it is too late.

Stand With Israel

America would not be in the place it is in if we would Stand With Israel. Change must take place where Israel is concerned or the worst is yet to come.

President Obama, the American people understand that a nuclear armed Iran is an existential threat to our ally Israel and indeed to the whole civilized world.

Iran has stated a desire to wipe Israel off the map and kill Americans at any opportunity. The American people are calling on your administration to Stand with Israel in its efforts to stop Iran from obtaining nuclear weapons and provide support for the defense of Israel's homeland and people.

Look how quick our Nation changed on 911. This is because Israel and America are both on the demonic realms hit list.

Mr. President we call on you to follow these principles and never waiver in your support to our ally in our common goals of freedom and democracy.

Prevent Iran from ever attaining nuclear weapons capability Support Israel directly and indirectly if she sees fit to militarily remove Iran's nuclear threat. Encourage other nations in the Middle East to publicly oppose a nuclear Iran and denounce rhetoric and violence against Israel Support legislation aimed at strengthening the US-Israeli defense alliance

Israel will be right in the middle of the end of the world. We must stand with Israel.

God spoke to me that when America stated there were no weapons of mass destruction in Iran (during President Busch's presidency) there was weapons found but saying there wasn't gave a false peace.

Every President announces change is coming and the reason being is that is all that is left after they are done. CHANGE!!!

Mr. President, it is simple. A nuclear armed Iran threatens the stability of the Middle East, our allies in Europe and the entire free world. It is now more important than ever to clearly pronounce full support for Israel's security. It is time for the USA to lead the free world and stop pandering and capitulating to those who want to destroy freedom and our way of life.

Our President's sadly imperceptive declaration—announcing that any quest for peace between the Israel and the Palestinians "must begin with a return to the 1967 borders"—is a betrayal of our nation's historic and just will to support Israel against antagonists that wish to destroy her very existence. Such a proposition is a time bomb with internationally destructive potential; a tragic commentary on our leader and his aides sidestepping history to placate war-like political forces that do not seek peace but rather Israel's eradication as a people. Neither should it be overlooked by believers in God's Word that each step our nation takes in such a direction is a step toward certain self-destruction.

Believers across the United States need to rise up and speak! But let each one of us do so *NOT as a railing statement of assault!* Whatever opposing view or earnest plea we express, we cannot expect God to honor a hateful or disrespectful stance shown toward our nation's highest office. Accordingly, let each one of us speak out as a citizen, indeed, as a patriot speaking in the interest of our nation. Write pointedly and briefly to our nation's leaders with regard to the President's declaration: that it is unrealistic in light of history's record, and that it turns a blind eye to the realities that occasioned the present boundaries. Speak as one who is aware that the occupation of the limited areas the Israel Defense Force took at that time were few and select zones; regions held to remove strategic positions and vulnerable situations that had before been used to attack Israeli lives and homes. State what should be obvious: that to vacate those areas *before* peace measures are ensured would be to expose Israel to the same bombardment and incursive activity that preceded the areas involved being occupied?

The occupied areas are defense measures; they injure or threaten no one. In fact, they significantly reduce or remove space for anti-Israel provocation to disrupt the peace which everyone seeks, and which the Israel Defense Force is positioned to help maintain for the benefit of all in the

Middle East. Let Americans speak ... speak by the millions to stand with Israel! To do so is NOT a posture against the humane and just treatment of Palestinians. Rather, it is to speak for justice based in history's truth and for all humanity—in the Middle East and around the world.

Our present circumstance risks disastrous exposure to the clarity of God's Word: that any who posture themselves against the Jews or Israel risk the awful consequences of such a stance. Let any who would overlook that issue be advised to inquire further of this truth which our loving and living God extends to us - truth which will not only make us free, but also make us instruments of His peace throughout the Earth.

As you read "**Why Stand With Israel today**".

I encourage you to take a steadfast and prayerful position of intercession before God's Throne. Speak to *both* God and man! Intercede by praying for the peace of Jerusalem.

Look at the cover of this book because this is the prophetic picture God showed me, if we don't rise up on behalf of Israel.

Psalms 122:1-9 A Song of degrees of David. I was glad when they said unto me, Let us go into the house of the LORD. Our feet shall stand within thy gates, O Jerusalem. Jerusalem is builded as a city that is compact together: Whither the tribes go up, the tribes of the LORD, unto the testimony of Israel, to give thanks unto the name of the

LORD. For there are set thrones of judgment, the thrones of the house of David. Pray for the peace of Jerusalem: they shall prosper that love thee. Peace be within thy walls, *and* prosperity within thy palaces. For my brethren and companions' sakes, I will now say, Peace *be* within thee. Because of the house of the LORD our God I will seek thy good.

Intervene by lifting a Christ-like, spirited voice to leaders in our land.

Intercession joined to intervention can penetrate any darkened strongholds that would blind leaders. "Eyes that see" will act in the light of justice and the facts of history.

We are living in a sobering moment in history that calls us, as believers in Jesus Christ, to take a stand with Israel. *We could be people of the last hour.* We are not to be passive in the face of prophecy; *we are called to pray* with passion, *to intercede* and *to minister* according to the words of the Savior who said it is not our task to speculate when the end will be. It is our responsibility *to do Kingdom business until He comes This is not about politics; this is about the Word of God, but the political ramifications are extremely dramatic.* Scripture declares there will come a time when all the nations of the world will turn against Israel. It is so highly conceivable this could happen in our time that it is critical to outline why we should stand with Israel today.

Standing With Israel

1. *Every believer is charged to make the Jews a priority in their value system and to render thanksgiving from their hearts for God's work via them as a people.*

Understanding the basis of the attention that we give to the Jews has to do with understanding God's divine order and things that God said. It involves a *people* and a *land*. Every believer is charged to make Jews a priority in their value system because God has.

In Genesis 12:3, the Lord says in the covenant He makes with Abraham:

Genesis 12:3 And I will bless them that bless thee, and curse him that curseth thee: and in thee shall all families of the earth be blessed.

This relates not only to a people (the Jews), but it also relates to a land (Israel). God will judge nations and deal with them for their decisions, just as He does individuals.

The Lord chose them for purposes:

Romans 9:4 Who are Israelites; to whom *pertaineth* the adoption, and the glory, and the covenants, and the giving of the law, and the service *of God*, and the promises;

The Adoption: God's divine choice of the seed of Abraham as a people.

The Glory: the manifest presence of God revealing Himself.

The Covenants: commitments that God makes:

The Abraham Covenant:

God says, "I will give you a people and a land, and through this seed the nations of the Earth will be blessed" (Genesis 17).

Genesis 17:1-27 And when Abram was ninety years old and nine, the LORD appeared to Abram, and said unto him, I *am* the Almighty God; walk before me, and be thou perfect. And I will make my covenant between me and thee, and will multiply thee exceedingly. And Abram fell on his face: and God talked with him, saying, As for me, behold, my covenant *is* with thee, and thou shalt be a father of many nations. Neither shall thy name any more be called Abram, but thy name shall be Abraham; for a father of many nations have I made thee. And I will make thee exceeding fruitful, and I will make nations of thee, and kings shall come out of thee. And I will establish my covenant between me and thee and thy seed after thee in their generations for an everlasting covenant, to be a God unto thee, and to thy seed after thee. And I will give unto thee, and to thy seed after thee, the land wherein thou art a stranger, all the land of Canaan, for an everlasting possession; and I will be their God. And God said unto Abraham, Thou shalt keep my covenant therefore, thou, and thy seed after thee in their generations. This *is* my covenant, which ye shall keep, between me and you and thy seed after thee; Every man child among you shall be circumcised. And ye shall circumcise the flesh of your foreskin; and it shall be a token of the covenant betwixt me and you. And he that is eight days old shall be circumcised among you, every man child in your generations, he that is born in the house, or bought with money of any stranger, which *is* not of thy seed. He that is born in thy house, and he that is bought with thy money, must needs be circumcised: and my covenant shall be in your flesh for an everlasting covenant. And the uncircumcised man child whose flesh of his foreskin is not circumcised, that soul shall be cut off from his people; he hath broken my covenant. And God said unto Abraham, As for Sarai thy wife, thou shalt not call her name Sarai, but Sarah *shall* her name *be.* And I will bless her, and give thee a son also of her: yea, I will bless her, and she shall be *a mother* of nations; kings of people shall be of her. Then Abraham fell upon his face, and laughed, and said in his heart, Shall *a child* be born unto him that is an hundred years old? and shall Sarah, that is ninety years old, bear? And Abraham said unto God, O that Ishmael might live before thee! And God said, Sarah thy wife shall bear thee a son indeed; and thou shalt call his name Isaac: and I will establish my covenant with him for an everlasting covenant, *and* with his seed after him. And as for Ishmael, I have heard thee: Behold, I have blessed him, and will make him fruitful, and will multiply him exceedingly; twelve princes shall he beget, and I will make him a great nation. But my covenant will I establish with Isaac, which Sarah shall bear unto thee at this set time in the next year. And he left off talking with him, and God went up from Abraham. And Abraham took Ishmael his son, and all that were born in his house, and all that were bought with his money, every male among the men of Abraham's house; and circumcised the flesh of their foreskin in the selfsame day, as God had said unto him. And Abraham *was* ninety years old and nine, when he was circumcised in the flesh of his foreskin. And Ishmael his son *was* thirteen years old, when he was circumcised in the flesh of his foreskin. In the selfsame day was Abraham circumcised, and Ishmael his son. And all the men of his house, born in the house, and bought with money of the stranger, were circumcised with him.

The Mosaic Covenant: The revelation of the law, given as a teaching means to lead us to Christ: redemption through the blood of the Lamb.

The New Covenant: In Jeremiah and Ezekiel, God says in words almost parallel: "For the time will come that I will take My law and I will make a new covenant with you, and I will put My Spirit within you."

The Greatest Gift: the wonder of the gift of Jesus to mankind. "God so loved the world that He gave His only begotten Son..." He gave Him through the Jews, and He came as a Jew. Jesus Himself, speaking to the woman of Samaria, said, "Salvation is of the Jews."

So Scripture speaks to us very clearly: *We're dealing with the roots of everything that has to do with the revelation of God to humankind.* The proof of this is in the very existence of the Jews as a people and the fact that they've been recovered as a nation. Today the struggle is over Jerusalem, over Israel, and over the presence of Jews and their right to have a land.

There are few nations willing to make an abiding commitment to stand by the Jews and Israel, but the Bible says God will honor those who do.

Our place in God's present order links us with the Jews as a people

When we put our faith in the Redeemer who came through the Jews, we enter into a line of those who have trusted God according to His revealed grace and redemptive purpose.

Scripture declares that, spiritually speaking, when you receive the Lord, you become a Jew.

Romans 2:28, 29 For he is not a Jew, which is one outwardly; neither *is that* circumcision, which is outward in the flesh: But he *is* a Jew, which is one inwardly; and circumcision *is that* of the heart, in the spirit, *and* not in the letter; whose praise *is* not of men, but of God.

Galatians 3:26-29 For ye are all the children of God by faith in Christ Jesus. For as many of you as have been baptized into Christ have put on Christ. There is neither Jew nor Greek, there is neither bond nor free, there is neither male nor female: for ye are all one in Christ Jesus. And if ye *be* Christ's, then are ye Abraham's seed, and heirs according to the promise.

If you are a believer, *you cannot be consistent with the whole of Scripture and take a position that is passive toward the Jews and Israel.*

God has made declarations regarding the land of Israel

Leviticus 25:23, 24 The land shall not be sold for ever: for the land *is* mine; for ye *are* strangers and sojourners with me. And in all the land of your possession ye shall grant a redemption for the land.

Deuteronomy 32:43 Rejoice, O ye nations, *with* his people: for he will avenge the blood of his servants, and will render vengeance to his adversaries, and will be merciful unto his land, *and* to his people.

2Chronicles 7:20 Then will I pluck them up by the roots out of my land which I have given them; and this house, which I have sanctified for my name, will I cast out of my sight, and will make it *to be* a proverb and a byword among all nations.

Psalms 85:1, 2 To the chief Musician, A Psalm for the sons of Korah. LORD, thou hast been favourable unto thy land: thou hast brought back the captivity of Jacob. Thou hast forgiven the iniquity of thy people, thou hast covered all their sin. Selah.

Isaiah 8:8 And he shall pass through Judah; he shall overflow and go over, he shall reach *even* to the neck; and the stretching out of his wings shall fill the breadth of thy land, O Immanuel.

Jeremiah 2:7 And I brought you into a plentiful country, to eat the fruit thereof and the goodness thereof; but when ye entered, ye defiled my land, and made mine heritage an abomination.

God is speaking to people in the end times that rise up against Israel. God is speaking of a confrontation that will take place in His land.

Ezekiel 38:16 And thou shalt come up against my people of Israel, as a cloud to cover the land; it shall be in the latter days, and I will bring thee against my land, that the heathen may know me, when I shall be sanctified in thee, O Gog, before their eyes.

Joel 1:6 For a nation is come up upon my land, strong, and without number, whose teeth *are* the teeth of a lion, and he hath the cheek teeth of a great lion.

Joel 2:18 Then will the LORD be jealous for his land, and pity his people.

Joel 3:20 But Judah shall dwell for ever, and Jerusalem from generation to generation.

Hosea 9:3 They shall not dwell in the LORD'S land; but Ephraim shall return to Egypt, and they shall eat unclean *things* in Assyria.

Zechariah 9:16 And the LORD their God shall save them in that day as the flock of his people: for they *shall be as* the stones of a crown, lifted up as an ensign upon his land.

When we talk about Israel, we are dealing with: A piece of property that God has made pronouncements about and God's people to whom He's given the land. It is a major issue with the Creator of all things, and it is non-negotiable. *Things that God has said uniquely about Israel have never been rescinded.*

Not only does the land belong to God, but also God has committed the land to Abraham and his offspring of Isaac forever.

Genesis 17:7, 8 And I will establish my covenant between me and thee and thy seed after thee in their generations for an everlasting covenant, to be a God unto thee, and to thy seed after thee. And I will give unto thee, and to thy seed after thee, the land wherein thou art a stranger, all the land of Canaan, for an everlasting possession; and I will be their God.

Isaiah 54:8-10 In a little wrath I hid my face from thee for a moment; but with everlasting kindness will I have mercy on thee, saith the LORD thy Redeemer. For this *is as* the waters of Noah unto me: for *as* I have sworn that the waters of Noah should no more go over the earth; so have I sworn that I would not be wroth with thee, nor rebuke thee. For the mountains shall depart, and the hills be removed; but my kindness shall not depart from thee, neither shall the covenant of my peace be removed, saith the LORD that hath mercy on thee.

The loss of governance by Israel through sin and dispersion has not altered God's announced commitment to make it theirs forever.

Ezekiel 37:1-28 The hand of the LORD was upon me, and carried me out in the spirit of the LORD, and set me down in the midst of the valley which *was* full of bones, And caused me to pass by them round about: and, behold, *there were* very many in the open valley; and, lo, *they were* very dry. And he said unto me, Son of man, can these bones live? And I answered, O Lord GOD, thou knowest. Again he said unto me, Prophesy upon these bones, and say unto them, O ye dry bones, hear the word of the LORD. Thus saith the Lord GOD unto these bones; Behold, I will cause breath to enter into you, and ye shall live: And I will lay sinews upon you, and will bring up flesh upon you, and cover you with skin, and put breath in you, and ye shall live; and ye shall know that I *am* the LORD. So I prophesied as I was commanded: and as I prophesied, there was a noise, and behold a shaking, and the bones came together, bone to his bone. And when I beheld, lo, the sinews and the flesh came up upon them, and the skin covered them above: but *there was* no breath in them. Then said he unto me, Prophesy unto the wind, prophesy, son of man, and say to the wind, Thus saith the Lord GOD; Come from the four winds, O breath, and breathe upon these slain, that they may live. So I prophesied as he commanded me, and the breath came into them, and they lived, and stood up upon their feet, an exceeding great army. Then he said unto me, Son of man, these bones are the whole house of Israel: behold, they say, Our bones are dried, and our hope is lost: we are cut off for our parts. Therefore prophesy and say unto them, Thus saith the Lord GOD; Behold, O my people, I will open your graves, and cause you to come up out of your graves, and bring you into the land of Israel. And ye shall know that I *am* the LORD, when I have opened your graves, O my people, and brought you up out of your graves, And shall put my spirit in you, and ye shall live, and I shall place you in your own land: then shall ye know that I the LORD have spoken *it,* and performed *it,* saith the LORD. The word of the LORD came again unto me, saying, Moreover, thou son of man, take thee one stick, and write upon it, For Judah, and for the children of Israel his companions: then take another stick, and write upon it, For Joseph, the stick of Ephraim, and *for* all the house of Israel his companions: And join them one to another into one stick; and they shall become one in thine hand. And when the children of thy people shall speak unto thee, saying, Wilt thou not shew us what thou *meanest* by these? Say unto them, Thus saith the Lord GOD; Behold, I will take the stick of Joseph, which *is* in the hand of Ephraim, and the tribes of Israel his fellows, and will put them with him, *even* with the stick of Judah, and make them one stick, and they shall be one in mine hand. And the sticks whereon thou writest shall be in thine hand before their eyes. And say unto them, Thus saith the Lord GOD; Behold, I will take the children of Israel from among the heathen, whither they be gone, and will gather them on every side, and bring them into their own land: And I will make them one nation in the land upon the mountains of Israel; and one king shall be king to them all: and they shall be no more two nations, neither shall they be divided into two kingdoms any more at all: Neither shall they defile themselves any more with their idols, nor with their detestable things, nor with any of their transgressions: but I will save them out of all their dwellingplaces, wherein they have sinned, and will cleanse them: so shall they be my people, and I will be their God. And David my servant *shall be* king over them; and they all shall have one shepherd: they shall also walk in my judgments, and observe my statutes, and do them. And they shall dwell in the land that I have given unto Jacob my servant, wherein your fathers have dwelt; and they shall dwell therein, *even* they, and their children, and their children's children for ever: and my servant David *shall be* their prince for ever. Moreover I will make a covenant of peace with them; it shall be an everlasting covenant with them: and I will place them, and multiply them, and will set my sanctuary in the midst of them for evermore. My tabernacle also shall be with them: yea, I will be their God, and they shall be my people. And the heathen shall know that I the LORD do sanctify Israel, when my sanctuary shall be in the midst of them for evermore.

Israel's present conflict is neither by their initiative nor perpetuated by racism on their part

The general attitude of the world today regards the Palestinians as the underdog, but *Israel is defending the land covenanted to them* in 1917 and established by the United Nations Assembly in 1948. The Palestinian goal is not to secure a homeland but *to drive Israel out altogether*. For the sake of mounting public opinion against Israel, surrounding, well-resourced Arab nations have never offered refuge to the Palestinians. The majority of the world doesn't know this, and nobody is bothering to tell them because sympathies are so overridden by other forces.

To stand with Israel is not to oppose Arab peoples or to oppose the rights of Arabs living in Israel

God has no disposition against *any* human being, certainly not Arabs who are the offspring of, Ishmael, the other son of His chosen leader Abraham. Standing for Israel doesn't require an anti-Arab stance and doesn't require us to be loveless toward other people.

Driven by spiritual powers that will not be satisfied until Israel ceases to exist

The forces opposed to Israel are not simply those of people who don't like Jews. We are caught in the stream of *spiritual forces* greater than humanity, forces that cannot be overthrown politically or by the power of persuasion. *These forces can only be broken by intercessory prayer where principalities and powers are cast down.*

The same spirit driving this hatred is equally opposed to Christians as to Jews

Just as Scripture states there are two witnesses that will be put to death in Jerusalem at the very end of time, there have been two witnesses that have stood for God throughout history: the Jews and the Christians. The hostilities and animosities are just as leveled at believers as they are at Israel, because there is a spirit in the world that is against all that is called God and everything about Him.

God as Creator - to Whom we owe our worship.

God as Judge - to Whom we owe our accountability.

God as Redeemer - Who has shown Himself through His Son, Jesus.

God as the moral Lawgiver of all humanity - to Whom we owe a responsibility in terms of our behavior.

Intercession with expectancy, and our support with promise

We are called to stand with Israel today because we could be people of the last hour. The Lord has called us to be people with moral and biblical conviction, walking wisely and knowing His Word. He will honor those who make an abiding commitment to stand with the land He's called uniquely His.

Psalms 122:6 Pray for the peace of Jerusalem: they shall prosper that love thee.

Stand Up for Israel

Equip yourself with reliable information, avoiding bigotry and disallowing "blind spots." Recognize the disposition of the popular press. Assess reports cautiously but not with paranoia. Become familiar with the basics of history in the Middle East, and understand the past century.

Accept with continuing faithfulness the Bible's call to *"Pray for the peace of Jerusalem."*

Psalms 122:6 Pray for the peace of Jerusalem: they shall prosper that love thee.

Genesis 12:1-3 Now the LORD had said unto Abram, Get

thee out of thy country, and from thy kindred, and from thy father's house, unto a land that I will shew thee: And I will make of thee a great nation, and I will bless thee, and make thy name great; and thou shalt be a blessing: And I will bless them that bless thee, and curse him that curseth thee: and in thee shall all families of the earth be blessed.

Prayerfully consider visiting Israel as a point of practical support.

Show friendship toward Jewish friends. Affirm that, as a believer, you stand with Israel as a point of your Bible-based commitment to God.

While acknowledging the terrorist habits of radical Muslims, be gracious to others. Take action because it's such a pivotally important time. Today, the showdown that we face is so close to being the nations of the Earth against Israel and whoever is left that stands with them.

The Lord has called us to be a people who will touch people and will stand with moral and biblical convictions for critical issues...and this is one.

We all need to be ready to Sound the Alarm concerning things that God speaks about. We have to pray for real men and women of God to rise with the sword of God in our mouth. We need to hear things that make us uncomfortable in our lack of truths being released in this hour. My heart is to see God impact all of these things. We can see God move in the White House. God said a couple times a year to release a Sound the Alarm. After each conference we will have what God released put into a book. We do things to release a new fire in the Church while we have our freedoms in America. We have been in Revival for over eight months and God said to stop and have a Sound the Alarm Conference. We did that because we knew the importance of releasing this. We continue in Revival but we also continue releasing the truth of God's Word because it's the truth that sets us free.

A New Generation

This is perhaps the most important generation in human history with the single exception of the era that witnessed the Lord's ministry, death and resurrection. These are both sobering and exciting times requiring our full attention and sincere responses as we function as spiritual messengers to prepare a generation of champions as vessels of honor postured for the Lord's coming.

God is rising up a new breed that will rise up in resurrection power.

2 Timothy 2:20, 21 But in a great house there are not only vessels of gold and of silver, but also of wood and of earth; and some to honour, and some to dishonour. If a man therefore purge himself from these, he shall be a vessel unto honour, sanctified, and meet for the master's use, *and* prepared unto every good work.

You my friend are supposed to be a vessel of honor. If you are being chosen by God in this hour; you are being cleaned out in preparation.

The end-time scenario is beginning to take shape and the players are starting to take their position in the dramatic unfolding of events prophetically observed by prophets throughout history. Hunger and desire to become vessels of honor is being imparted to those heeding the call to get ready. It is time that each person will respond with favor and give the Holy Spirit permission to fully clothe them with Himself and the revelation of His Word, making us the instruments of His warfare and "useful for the Master and prepared for every good work."

God is making you ready to be a warrior. God gave me a Word when I was young in the Lord that said; I'm getting ready to take you through a boot camp, I'm making you a soldier says the Lord. One year later I went through a ruff season where I learned to completely trust the Lord.

This generation has the exceptional privilege to live in the day when the Lord demonstrates Himself and His glory in ways never experienced in any prior age. The preparation of recent years has been to make ready a people for His own possession who will bear His image and exhibit His redemption. In order to carry the mantles of glory and power reserved for this company, we must have resident in us His divine nature and adorned in His garments of salvation and righteousness.

Isaiah 61:10, 11 I will greatly rejoice in the LORD, my soul shall be joyful in my God; for he hath clothed me with the garments of salvation, he hath covered me with the robe of righteousness, as a bridegroom decketh *himself* with ornaments, and as a bride adorneth *herself* with her jewels. For as the earth bringeth forth her bud, and as the garden causeth the things that are sown in it to spring forth; so the

Lord GOD will cause righteousness and praise to spring forth before all the nations.

Clothed in Truth

You are going to know the difference between those clothed in truth and those who are not. We got to get away from the pampered sermons. If I hear one more "my sin is ok" sermon I'm going to blow. There are too many preachers that preach it is ok just keep sinning. God put in His Word rules that we are to follow to the best of our ability. You cannot live in one way and then another.

There are garments specifically designed for our unique generation and profoundly adequate to overpower the spiritual darkness the Scriptures point out will permeate the time of the end. It is not because we are more deserving than any prior age, but more needy. Neither will it be because of any merits of our own but because of His loving-kindness and compassion.

It is because of the Time we are living in. Just as great darkness covers the Earth so shall God's Glory cover the Earth. God is pouring out His Spirit upon all flesh.

We are being molded and shaped to the very image necessary to carry these sacred garments provided by the Lord Himself. By them we will manifest His glory and taste the powers of the age to come. We are to be an extension of Him and His representation on Earth. To do so, it is imperative we allow the Holy Spirit to fashion us to be perfectly formed for the garments of the "overcomer."

How do we become clothed with garments of a overcomer? We have to be overcoming the things of this world. You must face mountains in your life and then overcome them.

Some people don't understand prophetic. If God speaks to you that you are going to have great faith; it means that you are going to experience some pretty big things in your life that will require great faith.

The Scriptures clearly outline, directly and through types and shadows, the consecration and sanctification necessary to become vessels in whom the Lord will find His rest and through whom He will do His greater works.

1 Thessalonians 5:23, 24 And the very God of peace sanctify you wholly; and *I pray God* your whole spirit and soul and body be preserved blameless unto the coming of our Lord Jesus Christ. Faithful *is* he that calleth you, who also will do *it*.

The Lord Himself will be profoundly present to accomplish this work. The Lord is our Provider, Healer, Banner, Sanctifier, Peace, Shepherd, Righteousness, Recompense, Defense as the Lord who smites, and the Lord of Hosts orchestrating the armies of God providing a canopy of protection around those who are His sons and daughters. All of His attributes will be on display in amplified form during our watch

Great Anticipation

We need a great expectation and anticipation in this hour. There is a flourishing sense of anticipation and purpose in the days in which we are living. The marked increase in the intensity and focus within many Christians relates to the birthing of Kingdom purposes in our nation and throughout the earth. Some individuals are beginning to experience a measure of increase in the anointing and various expressions of outpouring to quicken and prepare us for the next wave of the Spirit. There is an outpouring of the Spirit is being released.

I was recently allowed by the Spirit to witness some individuals being taken "behind the veil" and shown great and mighty things that have been reserved for the end-time. This invitation is for a remnant of people to go behind the veil.

Revelations 4:1 After this I looked, and, behold, a door *was* opened in heaven: and the first voice which I heard *was* as it were of a trumpet talking with me; which said, Come up hither, and I will shew thee things which must be hereafter.

The objective and commission of these individuals is to spiritually understand God's great mysteries and their prophetic application. The messages associated with these revelatory truths will initiate the process of awakening God's people to their high calling and create desire to be groomed for that purpose.

It is our prophetic proclamation to begin to fulfill Revelations 4:1 and Jeremiah 33:3, as many saints call upon Him that He will begin to show great and awesome things which we presently do not know. The truths associated with this reality are quite significant and provide the keys that unlock prominent mysteries of the Kingdom of Heaven. Those who are allowed this experience will be fully sanctified—spirit, soul and body in preparation for this weighty responsibility. One of the former leaders of the great Healing Revival commented saying, "many of the leaders were functioning with overdeveloped gifting with underdeveloped character." Of course that does not apply to all but it seems that history does support that position in all the revivals that have been lost. Nevertheless, that will not be the case in this generation preparing for the Lord's return. It is difficult to adequately express the importance of being clothed with the garment of humility and righteousness in the execution of this commission and the sharing of the great mysteries being imparted in this hour. Our spirit is fully redeemed and bears the righteousness of God. However, that righteousness must also be extended to our soul—mind, will, emotions, conscious and imagination. For most this is a process.

His Banner of Love

As my experience continued, the Holy Spirit revealed how the sharing of Kingdom Truths with the body of Christ was likened to the preparation of a great banqueting table being set by the Lord for His Bride. Seemingly, the "implements and banners" that were being revealed to this group somehow were utilized in the adornment of the banqueting table, particularly around the area that was clearly recognized as the "seat of honor." Naturally, these things are shown in symbolic form to illustrate truth that will help us in the hour in which we are living and the responsibility being delegated to us by the Holy Spirit.

One of the banners particularly emphasized depicted an image of the High Priest in all of his adornment with the breast plate, golden miter and other garments. When this banner was displayed, an audible voice spoke with clarity and determined purpose and stated "My banner over you is Love."

Song of Solomon 2:3, 4 As the apple tree among the trees of the wood, so *is* my beloved among the sons. I sat down under his shadow with great delight, and his fruit *was* sweet to my taste. He brought me to the banqueting house, and his banner over me *was* love.

There will be many who will be allowed to go behind the veil, to obtain and experience expressions of His Divine love that will transcend anything that we presently know. It will be a greater comprehension of His love and heavenly design for us.

John 17:26 And I have declared unto them thy name, and will declare *it:* that the love wherewith thou hast loved me may be in them, and I in them.

His holy zeal and love for us will supply the essential spiritual provisions necessary to see us through to our promises. This central truth is an emphasis of the Holy Spirit pointing us to a form of genuine unity with Him that will also birth in us brotherly love and fraternal affection. Jealousy and selfish ambition have no place in the joining of individuals and ministries for the purpose of pursuing a higher mandate and greater fruitfulness during the end-time generation. Throughout the church there is a relationally based alignment of people and ministries that will produce a much higher anointing and authority in the realm of the Spirit.

A Unique Day

One need only look at the evening news to discern the hour in which we are living clearly points to the many biblical prophecies foretelling and describing a day of profound significance. Just as the Bible describes, all things are being shaken so that those things which remain can stand under the scrutiny and pressure of the harvest generation.

The prophet Zechariah foretells a unique day known only to the Lord that is neither day nor night; a day in which light and darkness become apparent at the same time. A quite significant day in which individuals will become the light of the world displaying the bright and virtuous attributes of God Himself!

Zechariah 14:6, 7 And it shall come to pass in that day, *that* the light shall not be clear, *nor* dark: But it shall be one day which shall be known to the LORD, not day, nor night: but it shall come to pass, *that* at evening time it shall be light.

This day is so remarkable that only the Holy Spirit can make ready a company of people to meet the challenges and spiritual demands of this hour. As it is written, "at evening time it shall be light." This is the "evening time" of human history and the light of God is about to shine. Many of the events that have taken place throughout history have provided a rehearsal for the confrontation between light and darkness as the Holy Spirit orchestrates the training of His army. Likewise, our adversary is also providing polluted authority to those who have set themselves in opposition to the Lord Jesus and His end time mandates.

A Mandate

Clearly, there are many purposes for which we are being equipped and prepared. However, three notable divine mandates begin to emerge as our primary focus. First, our highest purpose and the one instrumental in allowing us to achieve all others purposes and mandates, is to know God as personally and intimately as He may be known. There is an open door and a call to come up higher to a place of fellowship and exchange with the Creator and establish friendship with God.

From that place of communion we begin to receive the unveiling of His nature and attributes that are not merely intellectual perceptions but revelation and comprehension of

His Person. The prophet Isaiah was given the great privilege of seeing heaven's design before the throne of God as Seraphim spoke one to another declaring "Holy, Holy, Holy is the Lord of Hosts." They were allowed to see with their eyes demonstrations of His majesty and authority and give expression to it. Their words began to fill the temple with smoke and Glory by witnessing with their eyes and expressing with their lips the revelation of God sitting upon His throne in absolute and perfect supremacy and sovereignty.

As the Seraphim gave Glory to Him and He received the Glory due Him, more of his Divine attributes began to be revealed causing an even greater expression of praise and Glory. This Kingdom exchange and heavenly design continued filling the atmosphere with the Glory and illumination of God until the entire temple was saturated with the appearance and revelation of His Glory. That is the order of Heaven that is to be transferred to the earth providing the second end-time mandate: to create an atmosphere on the earth that is consistent with His nature and character in which He can dwell. If we can fulfill this mandate, all the other purposes and desires for which we long will naturally be established and achieved by His Presence and anointing resting in us. We must likewise become the instruments that create a similar atmosphere on earth so He can tabernacle among us and accomplish all that He has foretold for this generation.

The third mandate for winning the lost and healing the sick will inherently take place because of the evident Glory of God resting on the Lord's friends because of the close encounters they have with Him. We are given the incredible opportunity in this generation to function under the principles of the Kingdom of Heaven and experience intimacy with God and demonstrate the power of the age to come.

Lift Up Israel

We must lift Israel up more than ever before. And the Spirit of the Lord says, now watch, as each one comes in and they try to speak against Israel, they try to speak against My people – even the Christians, the – God says, I will bring every one down. For I have said I will protect Israel and I shall change Egypt. There are enough people in Egypt at this very moment praying to Yeshua, and God says, you watch how I'll take the Christians –I'll take those who are praying and I'll cause it to infiltrate, infiltrate until they say, "What is happening to Egypt because it seems like it's becoming Christ-like or Christian." And God said it shall be so that there will be confusion. But let them speak against My Israel, let them rise up against My people and I shall topple each one until I set up – I set them up as a righteous people and I allow Yeshua to be sung in the streets and it shall be an example to the Middle East. And I can do it and I will do it for the sake of My Son, Christ, and the sake of Israel, says the Lord.

God is lifting up Israel and those who lift up Israel.

Restoration of Israel and America

As God raises up Israel so shall He restore America. This only happens when we stand in the gap for Israel. We want to see the restoration of the fortunes of Zion! We want to see the restoration of the fortunes of Israel! We want to see in this nation the restoration of the fortunes of America. What God has given to ecclesia, His church, to His people - we demand that there be a restoration of the fortunes of the people of God, of us. Today, that's a word. I just heard something that struck my heart."

It came from the Spirit. It came from the Holy Spirit but I'm speaking to the land of Israel. I'm speaking to the people of Israel right now. I'm telling the people of Israel that we're going to come and we're going to come with an attitude and we're going to prophesy from Galilee and Jerusalem and we're going to declare that the fortunes of Zion be restored – that God restores the fortunes of Israel, that God restores the fortunes of His people because it's time, it's time.

And God has something to say about abortion. God has something to say about the blood of these children that are crying out. I'm going to do something and many people are going to say, "How could this happen? It's a disaster."

But God says I'm going to shake the people of this nation and say enough is enough. Yes, abortions will carry on but one thing will happen that will cause a fight and a battle in the Houses and they will say we must come to a conclusion; there is too much killing. What are you talking about – freedom and the rights of women? God said what is the right of these children? I shall address this and My prophets shall prophesy it with others to declare that God will bring restoration and restore the fortunes to the people of America, says the Lord.

Let US prophesy to the soul of Central America, to the soul of North America, to the soul of the Middle East, to the soul of Asia, to the soul of South Korea! Now, Lord God, I pray that You would restore the fortunes, that You would restore the fortunes of Zion and that You would restore the fortune of Your people!

Some of you are being touched deeply by the Spirit right now. Some of your fortunes have been stolen! I didn't dream this up; this came as I was saying we need prophetic revelation – and suddenly I saw Zion and I saw Israel. Then I saw His people; I saw the church, and God said I want to restore the fortunes of My people. Some of you know what I'm saying; most of you watching know what I'm saying right now. Not for long! God said, and I declare to you today, God just said I will restore the fortunes of My people starting with Zion. And don't forget, we have come to Zion, the city of the Living God! I release that upon you now; I release that in every home and every life. Restore the fortune of Your people!

You know what I think happened there? I was taken away for a minute into the Spirit which doesn't often happen, but when it does happen, it's very clear – there's clarity, I should say. I was caught up and taken into Israel, just for that moment, and I saw the words written, "restore the fortunes of Zion" – and when I read that, I realized God is not finished with Israel; God is not finished with His people. God is not finished with America; God is not finished with England; God is not finished with Mexico, I promise you.

No Further Delay

God is speaking that there will be no more delay to those things His Body has been believing for. While I was praying I had a vision, and I don't say that lightly, I saw these words – there's an open book then there's an open heaven. And I was frustrated because I couldn't understand what was written. I saw it a few times, and then I prayed.

The Lord said to me, "Unless I proclaim something, it can never be understood." In other words, I have to speak first for it to be understood – and then He did speak and I'm going to share just three or maybe four things today of what I saw and I was able to interpret and I'm allowed to utter.

The first thing I saw was NO FURTHER DELAY. God took me into the Book of Revelation and Daniel and gave me a prophetic insight into it. I'm not going to share that today. I know what NO FURTHER DELAY means now. Once He took me to the Holy Scriptures, it all made sense and I know the time we're living in – and the time we're living in is the time of a global move of the Spirit reaching every nation of the earth. You may have heard that before but I'll take you to the Book of Revelation now that I understand what those words were. The fourth thing I saw was the description of a specific angel. I will put the Scriptures behind everything I saw in that book. There were 50 or 60 things written; I've only got four or five of them, but I'm pressing in and I'm praying and I'm fasting and He's showing me. I saw NO FURTHER DELAY, THUNDER, RAINBOW, and then a description of an angel that was called MIGHTY.

Increase Intercession

What does living the life of an intercessor look like? What would life look like if we postured ourselves as "victorious ones" and declared the heart of God into this natural realm?

When we yield our lives before Christ in prayer, He is then able to impart to us His heart of intercession. Inspired intercession is knowing God's plans and desires and declaring His will until it comes to pass. We can never give up or lose hope. Instead we stand on His promises and prophesy them into the unseen realm until they become reality in the natural realm.

Matthew 21:22 And all things, whatsoever ye shall ask in prayer, believing, ye shall receive.

If God has given us a blueprint of something, then we must have the faith to believe it will happen. We must stop believing by what we see, but believing by what God has showed us.

Communion with God

Prayer is one of the greatest spiritual resources at our disposal. Prayer is a way of communication with the Lord. Through prayer we are able to confess our sins, pray for the sick, bless others, and give thanks; communion with God is more fully facilitated by being personal with the Lord. But most importantly it is a way for us to express God's heart.

1 John 5:14, 15 And this is the confidence that we have in him, that, if we ask any thing according to his will, he heareth us: And if we know that he hear us, whatsoever we ask, we know that we have the petitions that we desired of him.

When we are in that place of intimacy with God, we can hear His heart. We are able to feel what He is doing and the season He is bringing us into. He is able to show us the things of the future and from that place decree them with greater authority. The time is crucial for us to begin to speak the hidden things of the Lord into existence, even if at the time we are experiencing difficulty and hardships. We are called to live a victorious life speaking as though our Father is speaking.

Mark 11:24 Therefore I say unto you, What things soever ye desire, when ye pray, believe that ye receive *them,* and ye shall have *them.*

That is a clear statement! When our relationship is secure in Him, our desire would only be to ask those things according to His heart and purpose.

Overcoming in Prayer

For me, at times a strong prayer life has been a struggle. I have a tendency to be preoccupied with my "to do" list. I would often spend my prayer time going down my everyday list of prayers. I was familiar with my routine prayer life, but I was missing out on the best part, listening to Him and being still and available to hear what He is saying. He has taught me through this process to clear my mind, call my spirit to attention and put my focus on Him. It is like breathing in the breath of God.

Prayer is not just about asking for things, although there is a place for that, there is much more to prayer. Prayer is being near God and coming before Him with an open heart. It is a place of opening our spiritual ears to hear Him and meditating on His Goodness. It is declaring who He is and the power of His great glory. He is the Kings of Kings and Lord of Lords; He is the Prince of Peace, the Son of God; He is the Messiah. Imagine how much the enemy trembles every time you say those words, and how much more in love with Him you become.

The Hidden Life

I believe a powerful prayer life is such a struggle because the enemy knows it is a key that draws us closer to the Lord. The Bride of Christ is to have Bridal intercession. I love the story of Esther where she was hidden away for 12 months in preparation for being presented before the King. It is amazing how she presented her case before him by trusting that his love for her would sway him into agreement with her noble request.

That is the mantle of the Bride of Christ! His great love for her will compel Him towards her righteous prayers. But we must first draw close to Him and have our hearts transformed into His. Our ultimate goal is be like Him and do the works He did. That is my deep desire. Along with being perfected as we enter into a place of rest in the presence of His Glory.

I believe living as a Bridal intercessor is knowing who you are without doubt or fear. We are Sons and Daughters of God by his amazing grace. We have the blood of Jesus flowing through us. By His blood we overcome the darkness of this world. I believe far too many in the church have limited themselves and limited God. Although many may not feel as though they are called and equipped to this deep intercessory ministry, we must be reminded of the Spirit's admonition in Colossian 1:27:

Colossians 1:27 To whom God would make known what *is* the riches of the glory of this mystery among the Gentiles; which is Christ in you, the hope of glory:

Christ in us is our hope of Glory. I love how someone once said, “God does not call the qualified, He qualifies the called.” That is so true! When we are weak, He is strong.

2 Corinthians 12:9, 10 And he said unto me, My grace is sufficient for thee: for my strength is made perfect in weakness. Most gladly therefore will I rather glory in my infirmities, that the power of Christ may rest upon me. Therefore I take pleasure in infirmities, in reproaches, in necessities, in persecutions, in distresses for Christ's sake: for when I am weak, then am I strong.

A New Model

Many of the old models are being put away, for this is the hour to stand in faith and prophesy the new things to come.

Isaiah 43:18, 19 Remember ye not the former things, neither consider the things of old. Behold, I will do a new thing; now it shall spring forth; shall ye not know it? I will even make a way in the wilderness, *and* rivers in the desert.

We know we have the victory over sin, death, and the darkness of this world. There is no way we are losing this battle because the Lord provided the victory through the cross. Even when things are hard, we must praise His name because what the enemy intended for evil God will turn to our good.

James 1:2-4 My brethren, count it all joy when ye fall into divers temptations; Knowing *this,* that the trying of your faith worketh patience. But let patience have *her* perfect work, that ye may be perfect and entire, wanting nothing.

The more we go through, the more we overcome, and the more we overcome, the greater our authority becomes. We are made perfect and complete and lacking in nothing. I believe God allows us to go through hard times because He has given us the grace to overcome it and will then give us Kingdom authority.

1 Corinthians 10:13 There hath no temptation taken you but such as is common to man: but God *is* faithful, who will

not suffer you to be tempted above that ye are able; but will with the temptation also make a way to escape, that ye may be able to bear *it*.

The Lord is a God of justice. Once a thief has been caught he must restore sevenfold. With this biblical principle, the enemy would have been better off leaving us alone.

Teach us to Pray

Luke 11:1 And it came to pass, that, as he was praying in a certain place, when he ceased, one of his disciples said unto him, Lord, teach us to pray, as John also taught his disciples.

This has been my prayer, " Lord, teach me how to pray". I do not want to pray in my old ways, asking and begging. I want to come before Him as His Bride, drawing near to Him in a deep place of intimacy and just BE. When we are near Him, He is able to dwell in us more fully. From this posture everyone we encounter will be impacted by His Presence in us.

Be encouraged to know who you are in Christ; the power that is flowing through you and your authority over sickness, distractions, or other issues of life. Our body is the temple of God and we have the right to take authority over every area of it- spirit, soul, and body. It is my prayer that every person hearing this message would be encountered by God on a deeper level and that your prayer life would be transformed into living in a place of victory. May your intimacy with Christ grow stronger than ever with a sweet desperation for more of Him and the fulfillment of Jeremiah 33:3:

Jeremiah 33:3 Call unto me, and I will answer thee, and shew thee great and mighty things, which thou knowest not.

Re-Election of Barack Obama

I've prophesied about many of our last presidents. Sometimes it is good and sometimes it's not. Any time I vote for the President of the United States; I look at three important keys.

1. Abortion (should be pro life)
2. Same Sex Marriage (homosexuality is an abomination to God)
3. Freedom of Religion (we should have our freedoms)

It's about lining up with God's Word.

Before the election, there were prophecies released that **President Obama would be defeated and Jesus glorified in the election**. I believe that the prophecy was accurate. We are not talking about the man but the spirit we are dealing with in America.

The "systems of anti-Christ spirit" that bound the nation will be broken ... Obama was re-elected, which has prompted that God's wholesale judgment is about to rain down on this nation because "God has put up with all of the mocking He intends to from Barack Obama": Obama in some ways has been looked to as an idol. I certainly believe America is and will continue to reap judgment. And I believe the fruit from the reelection of Barack Obama will be our most severe judgment to date.

Let us not forget that the political party Americans just voted back into power boldly favors abortion, homosexuality, homosexual marriage, and that they voted God and the support of Israel out of their platform. And. I might add, when God was put back in the platform after the potential fallout was realized. God is not mocked, however, and will have the last word.

Our economy will surfer greatly. The financial devastation and quality-of-care deterioration associated with socialized medicine will be staggering: more liberal, pro-abortion. Our Constitution disregarding. anti-God Supreme Court justices will be appointed (meaning more babies will die, marriage will be dishonored and immorality will be defended); Islam will be emboldened; our military will be weakened; and devastations from natural disasters will continue and perhaps increase. This is the short list.

The fact that Obama is a judgment, his policies will increase judgments, and this will be used by God to turn America is clear to me. What is not so dear is whether or not the outcome was controlled by God as a part of His judgment, or if He was giving us another choice and we rejected it. I cannot agree that because America had gone too far, God mandated the outcome. I believe He was still offering America an opportunity for grace. We chose judgment not God.

God spoke that Obama was as Belshazzar. This was the ruler in Babylon who saw a hand writing on the wall of his palace – as lie and his friends were mocking God. The ominous message written by the hand of God was, "You have been weighed on the scales and found deficient." The writing went on to say Belshazzar's reign would end. There will be many forms of the judgment of the Lord will take, but I am quite confident that God has put up with all of the mocking He intends to from Barack Obama, and that Daniel 5 is now his passage. I say this without malice or ill will, but nonetheless, confidently.

Tricks of the Enemy

God is revealing many of the tricks of the enemy. And I say to you. You have fallen off the horse one too many times and this last time you said I'm afraid to get back on again. But I say, mount up again, mount up again, mount up again for this horse will run faster than the enemies' that's been pulling you off. I say you've not had your balance in the past but you will balance yourself and become a skilled rider of My Word. So I say to you mount up again, mount up again and instead of being bucked off you will ride what I tell you to ride into your future! You've been like one who has had tethers attached to them and as you run forward you're pulled back, therefore in your Spirit you think you are a yo-yo in the hands of the enemy. But I say to you look behind you now and speak to what keeps pulling you backwards and once you do that, that tether will break and you will move forward quickly saith the Lord!

The part I heard was the Lord saying there is a wind that is blowing that will come and bring a shaking. And even the shaking that I Am bringing saith the Lord will be that which is good for you and it will cause you to see how My hand is moving throughout this earth realm.

For I Am coming with a wind and the wind is yes a wind from Me but it is a wind of rearranging, it is a wind that is bringing forth a shaking, it is a wind that is causing things to get into rearrange and move. For I Am bringing forth that Apostolic Move that you have been desiring, and I Am bringing forth that supernatural realm that you have desired to walk in for you are the people that I Am shaking saith the Lord. And a fresh wind is coming and it is a wind that will blow you into My purposes and My plans even before the foundation says the Spirit of the Lord. And I say to you it has been My desire for you to shift into new ways. And I say because it is my desire for you to shift into new ways, I have determined to go on the warpath, so that the warpaths of past seasons can be re-aligned. I say if I allow warpaths from last season to remain in the earth, destruction will continue. Therefore I must go on the warpath to lay out old structures, so that a new path of My grace can rise at what I longed built can be built. So I say to you I have now come on the warpath to change the paths of war that have been established in this land. And I heard the Lord say, align to the north, align to the North, align to the North, align to the North for there is a glory that I desire to rise up out of the North that you have not yet seen. But the Lord says it's going to take an alignment, the Lord says so turn, turn, even now turn, align yourself with the North. The Lord said I'm changing even a state structure. I'm changing into even an independent structure of the States and I'm aligning States even in new ways. And the Lord says there is a new arrangement that you are going to begin to see form, there are new alliances that you're going to begin see form. And the Lord says it will be protected alliances and alliances for the future. And the Lord said because of alliances I will demonstrate the power of agreement in the earth and I will bring a new glory over the land. And the Lord said this is the day that I spoke to you about; I will lay waste the mountains and hills, dry up the vegetation, I'll make the rivers coastland, I'll dry up the pool, posts and I will bring the vine by the way that they did not know. I will lead them in paths they have not known, I will make darkness light before them and crooked paths straight. Lord we thank You for this new path, we thank You Lord that darkness becomes light before us.

Now I hear the Lord saying this to us that certain things in your bloodline and in your life have been warpaths. In other words they just constantly end up in the same old warfare structure and the same old warfare strategies and the same old warfare cycles. God says if you will align with Me I will break the structure of warpath that has been set against you! For the Lord says that you don't know this path it's not in you. This path is in Me so today I Am cutting a path that you have no knowledge of trust and move with Me.

Now hear, I want to tell you I've never heard a word like this before you need to understand there is a path of war coming down from Heaven on your behalf that will cause you to get on a path of victory and triumphant above the warpaths of your past. For I would say to you just like when

My people came out of Egypt I was the cloud by day and the fire by night. And since I have established the fire by night in My Garden I say to you I Am the fire by night inside of you. So do not fear that you will not be able to find that path but line up with the fire by night.

Now I hear this that's why the Lord told me to come up. We have to hear the sound that God is bringing down right now. Get out of your minds get up into a new place because it's like the path for our future has been hidden and it's like God is saying I will lay out level after level after level until your path rises and you step into it! Decree right now you will step onto the path that will bring you victory in days ahead!

God is saying this today to us and say I have determined to go on warpath until that war path that has overtaken you in past seasons and removed your testimony is broken and your new path rises up. As we were worshipping I'm just seeing as we're singing and as we're singing the songs about, about freedom and breaking forth and opening wide and not to, we're too alive to stand still and no weapon formed against us shall prosper I'm seeing the leaves that are on the trees on either side of the stream of God. And I'm seeing that as the leaf is torn open that an oil of healing is flowing out.

I say to you I'm sending a river down from Heaven and My River is filled and full of life and wherever this river flows the leaves of the trees will begin to be filled in ways they've never been filled before and the colors of seasons will begin to change and trees that couldn't blossom in one season will blossom in another season. And I say to every leaf will be filled with a supply of life. I say to you there are many leaves that are walking dead among the earth and now I'm ready to loose a river that will produce life in those leaves and as those leaves begin to bud forth and break forth and are torn forth they will pour out and oil that has never released or been released for the time called now. I say a new oil of healing is forming and a new generation will bring forth the healing leaves.

I heard the Lord say that if we will come as those that are planted in the Living Water, if we will make our home by the revelation by the wine that is flowing down the river, the new nurturing that's coming through the river, whether the waters are going fast or slow, we will be nourished by the revelation. We'll grow and we'll get tall. He never meant for us to languish in the river, to ride in the river, to stay steady in the river. He sent the River of Life for us to grow and to get taller and to produce life and fruit.

So Lord we say that we're going to stand in the Living Waters we're going to take everything that You release in life, we're going to produce fruit, we're going to have leaves and everything we touch, everything we bump up against its going to release the oil of all of Your anointing and Your joy and Your grace to ourselves and to everyone around us Lord! And the Lord would say My Eye is watching you but now I will begin to direct you in a way that you will know that the path before you is being lit. I say to you I've been watching and nothing you've done has escaped from My Vision. But I say to you, now I will begin to order your steps. In ordering your steps I will begin to lead you through and into a place you've not been. My Voice will speak over you and the path that's been crooked will began to straighten out. I say look for your straight path and on this path is a four-fold anointing and return for you. I say My Eye is on you, now you will hear My Voice and hear My Word coming from behind you telling which way to step. You will come to a door where you're at the end of your strength and you will command the door to open. And on the other side of that door will be the strength and the might and the power of God. You will come to the door when you are at the end of your faith and you will command the door to open and it will be the faith and the power of God. You will come to the door when you are at the end of your health and it will be the Healer God and you will command the door to healing to open.

We say that this is the Season where our Kinsman Redeemer will redeem and open every door before us.

The Lord would say to you, why do you continually war with the handle on the door? Truly the enemy has set that handle as a distraction, look and see, all you have to do is push the door and the door will open unto you. Am I not the God that changed the garment of the Priesthood so that they could enter into the Holy of Holies? And yes I Am the God that has opened the door unto you. So push, push, push and come in, come in, come in, come in because I welcome you in My Throne Room in a new way. So yes today is the day, let go of the distraction because it is designed to ensnare you and raise your hand and push and see what is opened before you in My Holy Name. And the Lord says that handle is you asking Me how can I do this? I don't know how to do this I'm not sure how to work this? I don't know how to put my hand on that? And the Lord says don't ask that question any longer. The Lord says just push, step into what I've ordained for you. The Lord says there are no questions there are only answers for you ahead! And I just sense this morning the Lord was saying to us that this is not a time to try to close what I'm trying to open. And God says this is a time you're going to have to wait, because God said, I'm opening some doors for you and if you will be patient and if you will wait upon Me I'll give you access through that door. And God said this is not the time to try to close what I'm opening because you are in a new season and in the last season that that was closed and that was locked up to you God said you are not in that season be willing to let Me open those doors. And no it won't just be one door but this is a season of multiplication. And I say I Am multiplying the doors that I'm going to open for you.

God said do not get distracted and look in only one direction but I'm causing you to be so alert I'm causing those dreams and visions to arise within you. And God said even those dreams and visions from the past where the doors were closed watch Me as I give you access and I give you multiple doors that you will walk through in this new season.

We are entering a seven years of God's blessings. And now we're entering another season of marriages so I don't know what that means. But I do know that it means something and I know that year eight is gonna bring a lot of new things.

Yes because when one season ends a new one begins. And so get ready for that new beginning, get ready for that fresh start, get ready for that increase.

The Table of the Remnant

Over the last year God has released many Words concerning a remnant of people He is going to use. The Holy Spirit says that unless you hear the Father's voice, and come to know Him well, your lamp is not full and you will be out of oil when Jesus returns for His bride. The Holy Spirit is already moving on the earth. He has an army following Him, as He confronts the god of this world, Satan. The Holy Spirit is coming against all the strongholds and the works of that blasphemer. The Holy Spirit's purpose is to prepare the earth for the return of Jesus, which is coming soon. We are all called to join the Holy Spirit, and be led by Him. For this reason, the Father has a table set in the heavenlies. It is His table, and it is set with food; prophecies, teachings, an understanding of His will. Come and join His Holy Spirit at this table.

God says, "You do not know Me. As Abraham knew Me, you do not know Me. As you know your father and mother, you do not know Me. You may have gone to church all your life. You may have read the Bible through many times, yet you do not know Me. Come and seek Me and you will find Me. Come and know Me, and do My will in this age, the Age of the Return of My Son, Jesus."

There is an apostle and a prophet from the Father at the Table. The apostle teaches, and the prophet speaks directly from the Father concerning everything He shows. The Father wants you to know that His servants speak for Him, and therefore can be trusted to bring across the truth from Him, but in particular He desires you to come to know Him. We speak boldly in His name, because He tells us to do so, and He has given His Holy Spirit for this day and hour.

One Nation Under God at War describes the Holy Spirit's actions and purposes in the war against evil, which is being waged on the earth. This war will end with the return of Jesus to the earth. God is speaking to His remnant of people what the Holy Spirit is saying and doing, and what He wants His army to do.

The Table of the Remnant describes the origins of the Table of the Remnant, which is a fellowship in the Spirit, and a gathering of His servants. The Table is set. The Father says to you, "Come and dine. Come and hear Me and know Me, while it is still day. Come and get enough oil in your lamps".

Jesus is Alive and Knows Your Name is the message from the Holy Spirit to the whole earth: You can know Jesus. When He made you, His intention was that you and He would know each other, and that you and He would talk about everything. Everything that is beautiful and kind and compassionate, hopeful and loving, you will find in Jesus. You need Him. We live in unprecedented times, fearful times. This writing speaks of who Jesus is and once you start this journey with Him, He will never leave you.

The Obedient Remnant truly love Jesus and will obey Him. Here in this section are pages for the remnant, who are the few who really do know the Father, and hear His voice. In this section there is teaching for His people. His remnant is His beloved Bride. How greatly He loves you.

The Fallen Church is what the Holy Spirit calls the disobedient church of this day. They grieve His heart, because they are shallow and religious and lacking in love, and they are unprepared in this hour of warfare. The Holy Spirit has been going around the fallen church, and coming to the people directly, He is coming to the remnant. May the church open their eyes, and repent.

The End of the World 2012?

The year 2012 many people around the globe are wondering if the end of the world is near. I don't think there has ever been such a widespread interest in this topic like there is today. And who can blame people for wondering, when you see what is happening to our world. The signs of the end are prevalent. War, famine, natural disasters, incredible and rapid increase in knowledge. Poisoning of the air and water. Birds of the air and the Fish of the seas dying in huge numbers.

The signs are **so strong** now and the evidence is so clear that any person willing to accept the truth can see that the end of the world, as we know it, is **near**. 2 Timothy 3:1-5 This know also, that in the last days **perilous times shall come**. For **men shall be lovers of their own selves, covetous, boasters, proud, blasphemers, disobedient to parents, unthankful, unholy, Without natural affection, trucebreakers, false accusers, *incontinent*, fierce, despisers of those that are good, Traitors, heady, highminded, lovers of pleasures more than lovers of God; Having a form of godliness, but denying the power thereof**: from such turn away.

These verses predicted a great moral degeneration in our society. 2 Peter 2:3, 4 And through covetousness shall they with feigned words make merchandise of you: whose judgment now of a long time lingereth not, and their damnation slumbereth not. For if God spared not the angels that sinned, but cast *them* down to hell, and delivered *them* into chains of darkness, to be reserved unto judgment;

Do we live in a day of scoffers? Most certainly! Talk about the end times and the majority of people, including many Christians will just laugh it off saying that "all things continue as they were from the beginning of the creation." in **PERFECT** fulfillment of this Bible prophecy above!

So lets look at just some of the signs from the above Bible verse in Timothy and apply it to our time and see if it tells us that we are living at the end of the world, just before the second coming of Jesus. Are we living in perilous times? There is no doubt about that. Let's just take one example of what is happening today. There are uprisings all around the world, with people protesting and rioting and governments toppling. The people are starting to see the power they have if they get together. And this is a very dangerous situation and one that will lead to the image of the beast being formed, which will bring on the enforcement of the beast's mark. And with the economy melting all around the world, with countries nearing bankruptcy, the world is becoming ripe for a one world currency, which will aid with enforcing the mark and stop those who refuse the mark from "buying and selling"

Revelations 13:16-18 And he causeth all, both small and great, rich and poor, free and bond, to receive a mark in their right hand, or in their foreheads: And that no man might buy or sell, save he that had the mark, or the name of the beast, or the number of his name. Here is wisdom. Let him that hath understanding count the number of the beast: for it is the number of a man; and his number *is* Six hundred threescore *and* six.

You will now see how Paul above in 2 Timothy is talking about our day. These signs of the last days are so clearly speaking about our generation. Do people love themselves today by putting themselves before God and other people? Most certainly. We seem to be more concerned about how we look on the outside, rather than how we look on the inside (our heart). Everything now is commercialized to the extreme to make people think about *ME, ME, ME!* If you walked down the street just 50 years ago, you would have seen the majority of people dressed modestly in smart, humble clothing, **covering** their bodies. Today if you do the same you will see the majority of people dressed in tight revealing clothing to make themselves look "sexy".

Take a look at the 1950's. Do you see a common theme amongst the people? They are all wearing modest, humble clothing that actually covered their bodies, which is what God tells us to do in His Word. Now go for a walk through your nearest town or city and see if you can spot the difference. And why is there such a big difference? Because people had much more respect back then, and were much more humble. Today, the television, radio, newspapers, magazines and internet are full of adverts to try and lure us into buying the next best thing, to make us look better than the next person. Yes, this is certainly a sign for the time we live in. And what makes this sign appropriate more for our day is the fact that it applies to the majority of professing Christians also! The church is full of people who have no idea what it truly means to worship God, and think more of themselves than they do of God and other people. Just look at America! The majority of people there profess to be Christian. So why is it that there are thousands of people starving to death everyday? Because professing Christians are too busy with themselves to worry about the needy. **And Satan has deceived the majority of professing Christians into thinking it is ok to spend the money that God has entrusted them with on THEMSELVES, rather than using it to help the poor and further God's kingdom**. Well, we certainly live in a covetous age, where people clamor after the latest and best things. And not only do we covet possessions, we also covet after other men and women, whether married or not. The majority of people today are seeking after worldly riches, rather than eternal heavenly riches.

Again, this end of the world sign also applies to the churches of today. **Just look at what the prosperity gospel is producing!** Professing Christians just in it for earthly riches.

Also, think about how many women are coveted and lusted after everyday, because of the tight, revealing clothing they wear these days. And not just on the streets, but in the churches also! And again, the television, internet, magazines, billboards, etc, causes us to covet and clamor after the latest things this world has to offer. No doubt we live in a covetous time like no other.

Pride was the original sin that caused Satan to fall from his exalted position in Heaven, and pride is the sin that the majority of people cherish in this world today. LOOK AT ME is the way people are today. Too proud to be humble before God and turn the other cheek to their fellow neighbor. Too proud to stop and help someone in need just in case others see them. And as mentioned above, the way people dress these days compared to times past is amazing! Tight, trendy, revealing clothes to make people look at them and like them. Driving the latest cars and wanting to live in the nicest homes. LOOK AT ME, I've made it in this world!

Let me give you a quote from a newspaper in the UK after the riots there in August 2011 ...

"You have a generation of kids now that don't respect their parents or the police ... When we were youngsters we were made to have respect for the elders. Now if an older was to slap a youth that kid is going to pick up a hammer."

This is one of the many signs of the end of the world, and it is pointing clearly to our generation. The youths of today go about in gangs having little respect for their elders and parents, and pretty much little respect for anything. And why is that? Because society today teaches them that there is no God. They have no idea what Christ Jesus has done for them, and therefore they do not have any future. So really, it's not surprising that they rebel!

Our Neighborhood

Currently in our own neighborhood you can see a great deal of children with rebellion every day. We have a large number of children outside until 10 or 11 P.M. in their swim suits parading up and down the street. The parents only stick their head out to scream that it is time to eat. These children are from 5 to 12 years old with no supervision. The children are all left home alone while parents go to work. There is bullying, smart mouths, cursing when they are together and no parenting. This is the day that our children need their parents more than ever.

Many of us are unthankful today because we have been so conditioned by the world to just take things for granted. Just have a think about your daily life. Are you really thankful to God for the many blessings He has bestowed upon you? Do you thank Him for waking you up in the morning? For feeding you? For providing you with a job and income? Do you thank Him for His wonderful creation? And most of all, do you thank God everyday for giving us His Son Christ Jesus? Do you contemplate that amazing sacrifice He made? Now if Christians are unthankful, then what are those outside the faith like? We certainly live in a time of ungratefulness. Spare a thought for those who DON'T have today!

There will be some people reading this that have great troubles and difficulties in their lives. But you CAN be thankful. Thankful that God has promised us a future, if we believe in His Son Jesus Christ, and follow Him. Now this sign of the end of the world is an amazing one. Do you know why? Because I only need to talk about professing Christians here. Go back just 50 years and you would find a world with Christians who were far more holy and humble than they are today. Many believe that we need not keep the Ten Commandments anymore, just as long as we "believe" in Jesus. And what does this lead to? A people who continue living in sin and being unholy.

Jude 1:4 For there are certain men crept in unawares, who were before of old ordained to this condemnation, ungodly men, turning the grace of our God into lasciviousness, and denying the only Lord God, and our Lord Jesus Christ.

These men have certainly crept into the churches and as a result the churches are full of unconverted, unholy people today, who have turned the grace of God into a license to sin! Much more so today than in times past. Churches today have become more like social places, theatres and concerts, rather than holy places of worship. Christians have lost the Bible truth about how to worship in Church. Christians seem to think that they will be saved IN their sins, rather than Jesus saving them FROM their sins. There is little effort today being made in turning away from sin and living a holy life for God. And if this is the state of the majority of Christians, then what is the rest of the world like? Yes, this end of the world sign is being fulfilled today. We are sure living in the last days.

Another great sign of the end of the world! Just look at how homosexuality is being pushed and accepted. The Gay and Lesbian community, saying that a marriage between same sex couples is just as sacred as between a man and woman. We are also now seeing churches accept **ACTIVE** homosexuals. And not only that, many churches are now placing these people in leadership positions! Homosexuality is being pushed through television also, with many programs portraying homosexuality as normal. This is all in complete disobedience to God's clear Word.

1 Corinthians 6:9, 10 Know ye not that the unrighteous shall not inherit the kingdom of God? Be not deceived: neither fornicators, nor idolaters, nor adulterers, nor effeminate, nor abusers of themselves with mankind, Nor thieves, nor covetous, nor drunkards, nor revilers, nor extortioners, shall inherit the kingdom of God.

So many signs showing we are **IN** the last days! We live in an age today where people will not take correction or rebuke for their sins. If you warn Christians for wrong doing, many of them will just say "stop judging me!" and will not take correction. Even though the Bible says that the

Word of God is to be used for instruction, correction and rebuke.

All scripture is given by inspiration of God, and is profitable for doctrine, <u>for reproof, for correction</u>, for instruction in righteousness

This day and age, people are CRITICIZED for being pious. If you are seen to be a good, holy person, then the world will sneer at you, being labeled as a "goody two shoes". The world is so full of sin today that it cannot handle people who are good. This Bible sign is applicable more for our day than any other before us, and shows we are living in the last days. This sign of the end is powerful just on its own! Do we live in a world full of pleasure seekers? Most certainly. Again, to fulfill this end of world sign, we only need look at the professing Christian churches. A great majority of professing Christians are lovers of pleasure more than they love God. They fill their lives with television, partying, socializing, reading novels, playing games, wasting time on social networks like Facebook, and God gets little of their time. The films, TV programs and music that professing Christians are happy to listen to today is just shocking! There is no distinction between your average Christian and a worldly person today. Should Christians listen to secular music and watch all the garbage that they do? No, not at all.

The programs and films that are watched by Christians today are an <u>abomination</u> to God.

Now, go back 50 years and beyond and this would not be the problem that it is today, because life was much simpler back then. How many Christian homes give time to worship God as a family everyday? Not too many I guess, because they are too busy watching their favorite TV program, or reading their favorite novel, or playing their favorite games. We certainly live in a pleasure seeking world. This sign of the last days is fulfilled in our generation. Now this is an end time sign pointing purely to Christians. And is it fulfilled in our day? Yes. The Christian churches are FULL of people who only have a "form" of Godliness. How many Christians actually LIVE the faith that they proclaim? How many LIVE according to the way laid out in the Bible? Not many, which is why Jesus said ... *"will I find faith when I return?"* (Luke 18:8). And which is why He said that only *"few"* would find the narrow way, as the majority will head down the broad way to destruction. Why? Because they loved the world more than they loved God!

Yes, there may be "revivals" going on around the world today. But many of them only have that "form" of Godliness and are not filled with the true Spirit of God. Anyone can rent a stadium. Put on an elaborate "Christian" rock band on stage. Say "nice" things to make people feel good. Draw many people through the doors and call it "revival". But do you know what TRUE revival is? **Turning away from sin and living holy lives for God**. The so called revivals happening today are nothing more than worldly excitement. There is no doubt whatsoever, that the signs of the end of the world in the Bible are pointing to our generation. Anyone can see the great moral degeneration that has happened over the past 50 years. The moral depravation of this world has reached such a point that we are now like Sodom and Gomorrha just before God destroyed that city with fire.

2 Peter 2:6 And turning the cities of Sodom and Gomorrha into ashes condemned *them* with an overthrow, making *them* an ensample unto those that after should live ungodly;

So is the world going to end in the next couple of years? Did Jesus return before the end of 2012? NO!

We don't know when, but it is unlikely time, because there are still some things yet to happen that end time prophecy reveals, like the mark of the beast being enforced. Once the mark of the beast is enforced, we will know that we are in the VERY last days, right at the end of the world. But please do not wait until that happens to get ready. We need to get ready now and live for Christ Jesus and the Kingdom of Heaven every day. Don't forget, none of us know when *OUR* last day will be. So we need to be ready everyday. Satan's deceptions and temptations are going to get stronger and stronger. So please seek the truth of God's Word in the Bible and start living for Christ Jesus. Take a look at 2 Timothy 3 again. EVERY sign that are given in those verses are specifically pointing to our day today. These are the signs showing that the end of the world is near. We ARE living in the last days, there can be no doubt.

2 Timothy 3:1-5 This know also, that in the last days **perilous times shall come.** For **men shall be lovers of their own selves, covetous, boasters, proud, blasphemers, disobedient to parents, unthankful, unholy, Without natural affection, trucebreakers, false accusers,** ***incontinent,*** **fierce, despisers of those that are good, Traitors, heady, highminded, lovers of pleasures more than lovers of God; Having a form of godliness, but denying the power thereof**: from such turn away.

Social Media Watch

I sometimes wonder if the devil doesn't take great pleasure in irony, in watching us turn ourselves inside out while missing the point. While the Church is on Facebook, and therefore at least hold to a tentative conviction that such is allowable for Christians, there are any number of reasons to raise concerns over it.

Privacy and the lack thereof, however, would likely be the last one I would raise. With Facebook's very public and controversial announcement of its change in policy with respect to privacy, that, however, is what has many Christians concerned.

How, I wonder, can a person take a technology that exists to say to the watching world, "Here I am. Come see about me" complain that the world is coming to see about them?

Anyone who wishes more privacy can find such easily enough. Don't use Facebook. If you already do, stop. We are in a moral uproar for all the wrong reasons. We are aghast at the owners of Facebook for daring to change their policy (which, remember, the original policy held out as at their discretion) rather than being appalled at ourselves for implicitly breaking the 8th Commandment. We think because we are a user of Facebook that such makes us an owner of Facebook, and so demand this and demand that from the real owners.

That said, here are some very real concerns I have about Facebook. First, has it become a god to us? When God commands that we have no other god's before Him He doesn't mean ranked higher than Him, but rather He means in His presence.

If Facebook is too needful for you, you may need to stop. Second, has it become a graven image? Have you confused its reality with real reality? Do you really think you have 200 friends? Third, have you taken the Lord's name in vain? That is, have you, in weaker moments, put a bad face publicly on your Christian witness? Are you laughing at your old sins with that old buddy from college or high school?

Fourth, is Facebook giving me the peace of the Lord, or agitating me? (And please note the very real difference between that peace that passes understanding and that "peace" we receive when we feed a habit, when we get a fix.) Am I jumpy when I don't get to log on?

Am I more keyed up after I've logged off? Fifth, am I honoring those in authority over me? Wives, are you failing to honor your husbands because you're too busy reading about your friends? Children, are you failing to honor your parents because you're too busy sending flair? Sixth, is this technology honoring to life?

The cyber world can be a barren wasteland, not because it is filled with pornography and gambling, but because it isn't real, because it is Gnostic. Seventh, are you loving your spouse on Facebook?

Is the rush of nostalgia from finding long lost friends encouraging you to be dissatisfied? Are you secretly looking for that old girlfriend? Are you already caught up in adultery simply by wishing you could be sixteen again? Or do you not know that Facebook can all too easily devolve into relational pornography?

The allure of porn is that you think you can have the joys of the sexual union without having to have a real relationship with a real person. The allure of Facebook is much the same. Eighth, are you stealing from your employer by not giving a full days work because you are moonlighting pr, simply because you are spending your hours at work at play?

Ninth, are you lying? That is, is the real you present on Facebook the real you? This technology has an insidious capacity to both hide reality and fool us into thinking we are both showing and seeing it.

Why are our updates all about our victories- I just made cookies for the family; My son just hit the game winning home run; rather than our failures- I just shouted at my little girl; I left my computer on the airplane and it's gone? Keep a particularly close eye on this one. And tenth, is Facebook encouraging contentment or resentment?

Are you coveting your neighbor's friend count? Are you jealous of how many "likes" there are for his posts compared to yours? And are you content with the real life you are shutting out while hunched over your keyboard?

Please don't misunderstand this little thought experiment. I suspect we could walk through the Ten Commandments in light of our church, and find many of the same temptations. That doesn't mean you should stay away from church.

It does mean we ought to be deliberate enough to know what we are doing, and why we are doing it. And deliberate begins by affirming that our own hearts are not just desperately wicked, but deceitful as well. We don't need to protect our privacy. We need instead to expose our sins to the light, the light of Scripture that we might repent and believe, that His face might shine upon us.

Christians and Social Media

Many Christian organizations in the beginning invited Christians "to join the network of relationships which the digital era has made possible."

But during this time of year, when many practicing Christians give up Facebook and more leaders advise churchgoers to keep kids away from social media 365 days a year, the Chicago Tribune reports: "Facebook is exactly the opposite of the Christian culture.

The warning is directed at families trying to raise their children in a wholesome environment. It indicted social networking sites for encouraging vanity and dishonesty by providing an outlet for children to create their own electronic version of reality. It also pointed out, for example, that acronyms such as PIR (parent in room), POS (parent over shoulder) and GYPO (get your pants off) can lead children far astray. Children are using these secret codes to manipulate parents.

Texting, instant messaging and chat rooms use a strange, new language that's filled with abbreviations and acronyms designed to quickly communicate and easily disguise a myriad of sex and drug terminology. It's beyond the comprehension of most adults.

Some of the abbreviations and acronyms have been created so that kids can continue their conversation with friends while a parent is watching over their shoulder, confident the old folks are clueless.

For example, if you saw your daughter sending the text message, "PAW GYPO & Ill GNOC later" would you know she just scheduled a time for a naked video camera session after you go to bed for the night? And what's more frightening than not knowing when your 13-year old keyed LMIRL in a chat room, it meant "Let's meet in real life?"

I looked into acronyms, abbreviations, phrases and lingo to look for on your kid's phone or computer. Some are outright disgusting and we hope you never see your kids use them. Others are harmless on their own but still important to know in context.

If you feel guilty taking a peek at your little darling's computer and phone, remember one thing: You paid for them.

These are mostly never used by teens but they are now creeping in as more will unfold. Social media is a playground for deceit and secrets.

Warning: many of these terms are offensive

Texting Abbreviations, Acronyms and other lingo

- 8 = Oral sex
- 9 = Parent is watching
- 99 = Parent no longer watching
- 143 = I love you
- 182 = I hate you
- 459 = I love you
- 831 = I love you
- 1174 = Nude club
- 420 = Marijuana
- 4Q = F*** You
- ADR = Address
- AITR = Adult in the room
- ASL = Age/Sex/Location
- Banana = Penis
- BJ = Blow job
- BOB = Battery operated boyfriend
- CBF = Can't be f***ed
- CBJ = Covered blow job
- CD9 or Code 9 = Parents are around
- CYT = See you tomorrow

- DURS = Damn you're sexy
- DUM = Do you masturbate?
- DUSL = Do you scream loud?
- F2F = Face to face
- FAH = F**king A hot
- FB = F*** buddy

There are hundreds more you can get online.

"God entrusted parents with the care of their children for one particular purpose, and that is to teach them the way 'to know, love, and serve God in this life and save their souls hereafter.' Everything leads us to think that Facebook fits poorly into this plan and was devised for a very different goal."

As an outlet for children to create their own electronic version of reality, Facebook is hardly World of Warcraft. When it comes to encouraging vanity and dishonesty," kids can get plenty of that at the gas station today.

This Chapter isn't pointing out all the dangers to kids that are unique to Facebook or even social media. There are much stronger arguments for quitting Facebook and frankly, the creation of weak arguments dilutes the valid ones.

Agreed, when unmonitored, Facebook can be an enormous time suck or worse. And parents should stay apprised of their children's activities, both online and off.

But kids are future adults, and as such, must live in this world. Facebook is very much a part of this world.

Facebooks rule is that a child must be 13 to be on it. How many children under 13 are on it? Even parents sign them up. At this time any child of my wife and I will not allow facebook in our house.

If social media is addictive and it's holding you back from connecting to God and your understanding of spirituality, then, yes, by all means, pull back. But I think that oftentimes social media is allowing people to be church in a way that is unprecedented in our culture today. In fact, we should figure out, how do folks use social media even more effectively to be church during this time is another way to look at it.

Health and Spirits

We have to understand some things. How many of us know that when it comes to health problems it can be a number of things. It is not just in the natural but also in the spirit. Some people can eat all the right things and still battle health problems. Some people gain weight and it's not always the lack of exercise and the food they eat. Understand we can't except to be healthy when we eat unhealthy.

All my life people have tried to convince me to get on the band wagon. They will drink health drinks and preach to everyone that will hear them. Just because something says all natural doesn't mean it is ALL natural. I can call marijuana and cocaine natural but it doesn't make it healthy. Just because everyone is doing it, doesn't mean we all have to do it. Some have given me products and it just doesn't set right in my heart. I ask God and He tells me not to drink it. If God said to me; talk about this there must be a reason why.

We can become so preachy about one thing that it brings us to living in fear. I can't touch that or I can drink soda. Anything in high volume is bad for you. Many are living their lives with fears of what they are eating. "God did not give us a spirit of fear but of power and of love and of a sound mind."

Everything that says it is good for you doesn't mean it is. We need to really seek God before we eat or drink. We are to do this without fear. You can't pray Lord let this Twinkie turn into a carrot on the way down.

God has been leading me for years and we need to get down to the basics and really want all natural; you can juice your own all natural juices. Let God be the Judge about what you eat.

Living Healthy

One thin you have to understand is that you can eat all the salads in the world and still remain unhealthy. We all have to get off of our butts. Exercise is a part of life. I'm not talking about the gym type of exercise (even though all exercise is good for you). I'm talking about working around the house, walking and getting away from the lazy mode.

We live in a day of remote controls, recliners, TV, electronic games, computers, social media and more. We can really get to a place that we don't even move. They have cup holders and refrigerators in chairs now.

Our joints, muscles, blood flow and even our heart work better when we exercise. One reason many never exercise is because they say they are too tired. If you exercise you get more energy. Many times when someone gets older and retires from work they may age rapidly if they don't exercise or even move as much.

God actually made your body to heal itself of many things. If you injure you knee and if you move it and stretch it many times it will get better. If you do nothing swelling and stiffness sets in and now you can hardly walk. We don't have to be fat to be out of shape. We all need to exercise somewhat to live a better life.

Removing Fears

For months in the Waves of Revival Outpouring in Belleville; God has been speak on this subject of fear. We are going to reveal many powerful truths that are sure to set you free. The Devil; though a small adversary, he's a crafty one. He plays on our fears, feeds on our doubts, and works with our misunderstandings. He doesn't care what it takes to see you fall, only that you do! Nor is he particular on whom he uses his methods, only that we fail, give up, and ultimately self destruct.

He is the father of all lies and uses your own fleshly emotions against you every time. Fact is, your attitude is the key to your successes, and failures. I would like to leave you with a few insights on how the devil works, and uses his power of persuasion against us. Here are four, of many tricks, the devil will use to throw you off track. The devil wants you to believe he has power over you. He has no power other than what you give him. He comes in with lies and suggestions. If you choose to listen and act upon them, he gains power over you. The fact is, God has given you power over him!

Luke 10:19 Behold, I give unto you power to tread on serpents and scorpions, and over all the power of the enemy: and nothing shall by any means hurt you.

This is the last thing he wants you to know. He would love for you to think that he is all-powerful and can do anything he chooses against you. Remember Job. God had to allow Satan to touch him. If Satan could even touch you without God's permission, he would instantly destroy you.

John 10:10 The thief cometh not, but for to steal, and to kill, and to destroy: I am come that they might have life, and that they might have *it* more abundantly.

When the enemy speaks to you, it will always be in the first person as if you are hearing your own voice. It will sound something like this, "I can't make it anymore, I've been doing so bad lately, I just feel like giving up." The reason this method is so clever, is that it's the easiest to believe. If he spoke to you in the third person, "You are so bad, you can't make it, you're a failure," you would know it was the devil at work speaking his lies, and you wouldn't listen. We typically get defensive when others bash on us, and he knows this. The Devil always checks your understanding of truth (God's word) to see how much deception will be necessary to defeat you. When he told his first lie to mankind in the garden of Eden he started out by asking, "Has God truly said, 'You shall not eat of every tree of the garden'?" We must know truth in order to defeat him and to protect ourselves.

John 8:32 And ye shall know the truth, and the truth shall make you free.

He will try to make you unsatisfied with where you're at, so that you won't care about where you're going. When we spend our time being ungrateful with where God has brought us from, we lose the power of our testimony. Why is our testimony so important? And why does he want to take the power of it away from us?

Revelations 12:11 And they overcame him by the blood of the Lamb, and by the word of their testimony; and they loved not their lives unto the death.

Our testimony defeats him every time!

ObamaCare Health Plan

"Should Christians Publicly Stand Against Obama care? YES!

Here Are Reasons Why"

Well, here we are, Christians sitting as frogs in the proverbial pot of boiling water. And now after years of seeing the bubbles, we're finally starting to believe and feel the heat. Will we finally leap out into the fight, or continue to get cooked in boiling apathy?

Have no other gods before me

Tyranny...it's when "man" oppressively rules over man, and puts himself in the place of God (more or less.) The essence of tyranny is that no absolute God created law or justice prevails and instead, only the will of a man, a group or party of men, or a majority or a minority of men. What the small minority of elected men did by passing Obamacare was put the state, themselves, over and beyond their sole duty as a ministers of justice, and put themselves in a sovereign position over the lives of Americans.

So how does that mean we are sinning against God by supporting them?

Yes, our rulers are sinning by their actions but so are those that blindly follow them without question (or action). By casually agreeing with this tyrannical rule we are choosing to obey men rather than God and acknowledging man's authority over and in the place of God. We can't be neutral. There are no grey areas.

Have No Idols

I'm sure none of us have little President Obama statues in our house — at least most of us don't … yet. However, agreeing to controlled healthcare and medical services with mandated cooperation by Uncle Sam is very close. Why?

We allow ourselves to be intimately connected with the state by allowing all aspects of our social, family, business and personal lives to become accustomed to leaning on the state for care and help rather than God.

When we do this, the God-given resources the Scriptures teach that man should use in order to provide for himself, things like consistent hard work and sweat, are principles that are gradually put to the wayside — or worse, never learned.

As with any socialist program, this creates a spirit of dependence, lethargy and apathy among the people, causing us oftentimes to prop up, expect and support the state as a providing idol, rather than the Church — God's true resource for "health care" — and the Spirit of God Himself.

Do not use the name of the Lord in vain

The ultimate blasphemy is doing evil in the name of Christ.

Listen to this quote, "Obamacare is a move that will ensure that the U.S. is attempting to live up to its religious values while complying with the teachings of Jesus Christ."

Do you agree with this quote? Unfortunately, I know some Christians that would agree with that statement. If you're one of these people, please don't forget that Christ doesn't contradict Himself. He also spoke against stealing, idolatry, murder, covetousness and lying. All sins that Obamacare is guilty of are also committed by association when we buy into this sort of "social gospel" mentality.

Remember, Jesus never taught to rob from one person and give it to another, or for a government to mandate laws that take from people who work – or don't work for that matter – and forcefully give their wages to other people. This is stealing.

The Spirit of Christ should cause Christians to give out of the goodness of their heart, not by mandated government force with fines for those that do not comply. If we support this, we partake in the theft by default.

Do not murder

With well over 2000 pages, it's no wonder this legislation is scattered with anti-life, pro-abortion measures. Despite what is being said, abortion will be funded by taxpayers through a monthly, secretive surcharge.

Americans will now be forced to comply and indirectly participate in the murder of children whether they like it or not.

Would you give a portion of your paycheck this week for a woman to have an abortion next week without saying a word? Chances are, you'd rant, rave and adamantly refuse to allow it to happen.

Why then will we passively submit knowing our tax dollars are contributing to the murder of babies? (Do I even have to mention that if we do, it's sin?)

What about the taxation associated with Obamacare? The power to tax gives you the power to injure and the power to destroy. This bill puts the state in even more of a violation of this commandment.

The taxes that we have in this country are, for the most part, unBiblical — income tax, real estate tax, etc. — and are against Scripture. God basically calls for a tithe and for a civil tax on "increase." The mandate of this bill is now actually being labeled as a tax, which will send many companies and small business owners out of business due to required fees.

Over taxing also promotes social revolution. Supporting or participating in a bill of this nature puts us right smack in the middle of this sin. Stand against it!

Do not steal

Over-taxation and unBiblical taxation is theft, and so is wealth re-distribution. For the government to force one person to pay for another person's healthcare – or anything for that matter, is theft, plain and simple.

Not standing against Obamacare is contributing to theft in more ways than one. Inflation also is theft. It's a system of false weights and balances, which is all over Proverbs and beyond. Will we contribute to inflation when we buy into Obamacare? You bet. Bigger government means more money to run the government, which means more debt equaling more inflation. Can we control everything the government does? No. Are we culpable for all of their actions? No. However, when we have it in our power to act and choose not to, we are accountable.

We must not get excited by handouts when the hand is unlawfully digging into our brother's pocket. Remember, the government only obtains money by taxing or inflating (printing money).

Do not bear false witness

This bill could be summed up as one big lie. Not to mention, it plunges our debt-ridden 15 billion plus economy into more debt in order to run the beast of Obamacare.

Lying is at the heart of inflation. In a nutshell, when businesses over-price undervalued goods and services to compensate for inflation, it's stealing. Investments are made and lost due to inflated numbers.

People or businesses cannot invest honestly or accurately with a government that continues to print money and devalue the dollar. However, this is exactly what Obamacare will do and is doing.

If we don't stand against this bill, we will be sitting back endorsing our government's lies while they profit by stealing from others. There's no in between. If we're for this bill, we sin against God.

Do not covet

When someone gets a handout, and then another, and then another, guess what? They grow to expect it. Generation after generation in the state of a covetous heart and a covetous nation. We're not to eat if we don't work, says the Bible.

What happens when you cater to a lazy employee? You keep giving them grace upon grace when you should put your foot down and tell them they either must produce or be fired. What happens when you enable an alcoholic? Do they get better or worse? Is tough love better than blind love?

We are enabling a lethargy that we will not be able to pull out of when we contribute to this bill.

The Bible teaches creativity, enterprise, freedom and dominion. Its teachings imply a spirit of entrepreneurialism and heartfelt giving, not mandated handouts that hurt and cheat others.

If you think enabling an alcoholic is sin, so is enabling a Nanny State. We must refuse to remain quiet. We have to stand up for Christ in these areas.

We Must Obey God and Resist Obamacare

As you may have noticed, each of the above represents a commandment. But what about the commandments (remember the Sabbath, honor your father and mother and do not commit adultery) you ask? I purposely left them out of the main line-up of transgressions caused by Obamacare to focus on the obvious, but the missing three are also violated.

For one reason, if you violate any of the 10 commandments, you've broken them all. Now, depending on your view of the Sabbath, a good case can be made that Obamacare also violates it, as well as the commandment of dishonoring your parents. The commandment not only warns us to avoid sexual sin, but also protects the family unit. Much can be said on how endorsing Obamacare disrupts, discounts and disregards the family as well.

With all of that said, if any church member, non-believer, pagan or saint were to cause you, your family, your church or anyone you know to break all of the above commandments, would you not stand against them and reprove them with the Word of God? Would you not exhort them to repent and turn to God's ways and not the humanistic ways and rule of man? Wouldn't you at least kindly ask them "why" and question their motives?

If your children were supporting such sins, would you sit down and lovingly speak to them? Would you alarm them regarding the consequences of such actions? How about some instruction on how to handle such situations? I would hope our pulpits will alarm the Church in the very same way this Sunday and beyond.

It's our obligation as Christians, pastors and preachers to be salt and light, and to reprove the works of darkness. There is no line of division, no place where Christ is afraid to send you to speak out.

John 16:7-11 Nevertheless I tell you the truth; It is expedient for you that I go away: for if I go not away, the Comforter will not come unto you; but if I depart, I will send him unto you. And when he is come, he will reprove the world of sin, and of righteousness, and of judgment: Of sin, because they believe not on me; Of righteousness, because I go to my Father, and ye see me no more; Of judgment, because the prince of this world is judged.

The ruler of this world stands judged! How else does God intend on convicting the world concerning sin, righteousness and judgment if not through His image bearing, redeemed people going into every sphere of the world by the power of the Holy Spirit?

We must stand and speak against this massacre of Obamacare and not be afraid of the consequences of what our church members, pastors, neighbors or government may think. Are you in? If so, resist this tyranny by refusing to partake in it, endorse it or be associated with it in any way.

Pick up your phone. Write, blog, email. Go to your statehouse. Write your Congressmen. Call the media. Vote biblical. Support godly politicians. Run for office. Do what

God is calling you to do. Take to the streets in protest and with the message of the Gospel of the Kingdom, proclaiming Christ's Kingship and His message of forgiveness. But let's not sit still; let's do something. Yes, let's get active for Christ and jump out of the pot. It's time we stand up, speak out and take action!

Christians Stand Up

Various voices within the Christian community are expressing differing opinions regarding the recent Hobby Lobby lawsuit, which involves the Oklahoma-based franchise craft store suing the Obama administration for its contraceptive mandate, as it goes against the Christian values of the family-run business.

"When the government starts coercing businesses to violate their religious, moral, and ethical values, that is a flagrant violation of our Constitution."

Hobby Lobby, currently pursuing an injunction from Obama's contraceptive mandate, has thus far been denied in courts, and was recently denied by the U.S. Supreme Court an emergency request to block enforcement of the mandate.

As The Christian Post previously reported, Hobby Lobby filed suit against the Obama administration's Health and Human Services (HHS) mandate that requires all businesses in the country to provide insurance coverage for contraceptives, sterilization and abortifacients for employees.

Hobby Lobby's evangelical Christian CEO David Green previously said in a public letter that he is specifically against the use of abortifacients, meaning emergency contraceptives such as the "morning after pill," but does not object to the use of preventative contraception, such as birth control pills.

"Being Christians, we don't pay for drugs that might cause abortions, which means that we don't cover emergency contraception, the morning-after pill or the week-after pill. We believe doing so might end a life after the moment of conception, something that is contrary to our most important beliefs," Green said in his open letter.

"It (paying for abortifacients) goes against the Biblical principles on which we have run this company since day one," Green has previously said.

Although many Christians are supporting Hobby Lobby's owners for staying faithful to their Christian convictions, as seen through the Jan. 5 "Hobby Lobby Appreciation Day" organized by Mike Huckabee, others are arguing that the craft store should follow government policy, as should all U.S. businesses.

"I'm still not seeing a cause for alarm here. The majority of the U.S. thinks women's healthcare needs should be included in insurance plans ..... I'm a Christian, and if I start a business then I expect I'll have to comply with all the government regulations that come with incorporation. I wouldn't expect special treatment for my personal religious beliefs."

Others question why Hobby Lobby has chosen to address the contraceptive mandate but not other morally questionable issues within government, such as the funding of wars in Iraq and Afghanistan.

"What I don't understand is why this issue is any different than someone whose religious beliefs say war is sinful being 'forced' to pay taxes that support U.S. military operations in Iraq and Afghanistan."

"Either we are morally culpable for paying those taxes, providing that health coverage, or we aren't. If we do incur moral guilt because of the actions of our government, surely the Hobby Lobby owners must believe they are incurring guilt in areas other than just providing coverage for this contraceptive. But they don't seem to be making a big deal about the other areas of morally questionable government behavior," the commenter added.

"You see, when it comes carrying high the banner of 'Biblical principles', I believe a company who wanted that to be their public persona would be extra careful to NEVER do business with the very people who go against everything they claim to fight for as Christians."

Critics contend this daily fine would easily put the crafts store out of business within the near future.

Still, Hobby Lobby announced in late Dec. 2012, after losing an appeal of its case in U.S. Supreme Court, that the company will continue to defy the mandate and not pay for abortion-inducing drugs.

Hobby Lobby is among dozens of plaintiffs that have filed suits over Obamacare, including Roman Catholic groups, evangelical Christian college Liberty University, and numerous other for-profit and nonprofit organizations.

About the Author

Bill Vincent is no stranger to understanding the power of God. Not only has he spent over twenty years as a Minister with a strong prophetic anointing, he is now also an Apostle and Author with Revival Waves of Glory Ministries in Litchfield, IL. Along with his wife, Tabitha, he, leads a team providing apostolic oversight in all aspects of ministry, including service, personal ministry and Godly character.

Bill offers a wide range of writings and teachings from deliverance, to experiencing presence of God and developing Apostolic cutting edge Church structure. Drawing on the power of the Holy Spirit through years of experience in Revival, Spiritual Sensitivity, and deliverance ministry, Bill now focuses mainly on pursuing the Presence of God and breaking the power of the devil off of people's lives.

His books 48 and counting has since helped many people to overcome the spirits and curses of Satan. For more information or to keep up with Bill's latest releases, please visit www.revivalwavesofgloryministries.com. To contact Bill, feel free to follow him on twitter @revivalwaves.

Recommended Books

By Bill Vincent

Overcoming Obstacles
Glory: Pursuing God's Presence
Defeating the Demonic Realm
Increasing Your Prophetic Gift
Increase Your Anointing
Keys to Receiving Your Miracle
The Supernatural Realm
Waves of Revival
Increase of Revelation and Restoration
The Resurrection Power of God
Discerning Your Call of God
Apostolic Breakthrough
Glory: Increasing God's Presence
Love is Waiting – Don't Let Love Pass You By
The Healing Power of God
Glory: Expanding God's Presence
Receiving Personal Prophecy
Signs and Wonders
Signs and Wonders Revelations
Children Stories
The Rapture
The Secret Place of God's Power
Building a Prototype Church
Breakthrough of Spiritual Strongholds
Glory: Revival Presence of God
Overcoming the Power of Lust
Glory: Kingdom Presence of God
Transitioning to the Prototype Church
The Stronghold of Jezebel
Healing After Divorce
A Closer Relationship With God

Cover Up and Save Yourself
Desperate for God's Presence
The War for Spiritual Battles
Spiritual Leadership
Global Warning
Millions of Churches
Destroying the Jezebel Spirit
Awakening of Miracles
Deception and Consequences Revealed
Are You a Follower of Christ
Don't Let the Enemy Steal from You!
A Godly Shaking
The Unsearchable Riches of Christ
Heaven's Court System
Satan's Open Doors
Armed for Battle
The Wrestler
Spiritual Warfare: Complete Collection
Growing In the Prophetic
The Prototype Church: Complete Edition
Faith
The Angry Fighter's Story
Understanding Heaven's Court System

Web Site:
www.revivalwavesofgloryministries.com

Global Warning

Lightning Source UK Ltd.
Milton Keynes UK
UKHW041623041219
354427UK00019B/5/P

9 781087 85140